THE COMPLETE BOOK OF
ABSOLUTELY PERFECT
BABY AND CHILD CARE

Also by Elinor Goulding Smith

THE COMPLETE BOOK
OF ABSOLUTELY PERFECT
HOUSEKEEPING

ELINOR GOULDING SMITH

The Complete Book of
Absolutely Perfect
Baby and Child Care

DRAWINGS BY ROY DOTY

HARCOURT, BRACE AND COMPANY • NEW YORK

LIBRARY OF CONGRESS CATALOG CARD NUMBER: 57-12369

PRINTED IN THE UNITED STATES OF AMERICA

To Bob

CONTENTS

1. The Baby—What Is It?   11
2. On Your Mark, Get Set—   23
    (including remarks on solid foods, walk-
    ing, teething, toilet training, and other
    insurmountable obstacles)
3. Table Manners   32
    (including a frank and open discussion of
    ketchup)
4. Discipline   40
    (how to protect yourself from the child)
5. Cleanliness   45
    (what is it? I've forgotten)
6. Developing the Ingoing Personality   52
7. Family Fun   57
    (including absolutely practical sure-fire
    suggestions for healthy, happy, whole-
    some, jolly, exhilarating, gay, cheery,
    invigorating, merry, and mirthful games
    for all the family)

[7]

8. Health and Hygiene   62
    *(including a frank and open discussion of
    such subjects as stitches, plaster casts, and
    the handling of unruly children who
    bleed)*

9. Sibling Rivalry   72
    *(up-to-date instructions for playing this
    game, including full rules for referees)*

10. How to Survive a Birthday Party   80

11. Heredity and Environment   86
    *(an absolutely scientific discussion, guar-
    anteed to relieve your mind of any further
    worry on these subjects)*

12. Look Out! Your I.Q. Is Falling!   92

13. Money Is the Root of All Children   98

14. Infinite Kittens in a Little Room   104

15. Never Send a Boy to Do a Boy's Job   110

16. Reading, Writing, and Social Integration   116

17. The Advantages of Having Children over
    Hamsters or Kittens   121

THE COMPLETE BOOK OF
ABSOLUTELY PERFECT
BABY AND CHILD CARE

ONE

The Baby—What Is It?

It sometimes happens, even in the best families, that a baby is born. This is not necessarily cause for alarm. The important thing is to keep your wits about you and borrow some money. Many women attempt to keep a baby without *any previous experience*, and may not even know what a baby is. A baby is, actually, something like a very small human being in appearance, and comes in two kinds boy and girl. If you are not certain which yours is, look at its blanket. If the hospital has wrapped it in a blue blanket, it is a boy, if in pink a girl. Sometimes the hospital may run out of one color or the other and use the wrong kind, but in this case they are supposed to notify you.

Once you know whether your baby is a boy or a girl, it is a good idea to give him a name. It will save endless trouble in later years when you want to call him to clean his room or mow the lawn. (He won't answer anyway, of course, but that's another subject.)

Picking the right name for the baby is beset with difficulties. There are so many to choose from that the new parents are apt to sink into a feeling of utter despair over it. If you can't decide and you don't happen to have a handy family name that can be used, literature and history are endless sources of handsome and inspirational names, like Calvin Coolidge, Benedict Arnold, Genghis Khan, etc. If the baby is a girl, movie stars' names are often suitable and lovely, like Rita Hayworth, Dolores Del Rio, or Marjorie Main.

However, the fact is that whatever name you choose, the baby, some years hence, will hate it anyway, and decide to have his friends call him Slats or Rocky, so the whole thing really doesn't make too much difference. If the baby is a girl however, you can give her a middle name, and as soon as she's old enough to talk, tell her that the middle name is her first name. Then when she's fourteen, and using green ink and putting little circles over the i's instead of dots, and complaining that all the other girls use mascara and eyeshadow for school and you're treating her like a baby, she'll decide to use her middle name for a first name, and everything will come out right after all.

When I mentioned that in appearance the baby resembled a very small human being, I meant just that. For it is in appearance only, and the resemblance is slight at that. The truth is that a baby is hopelessly stupid. He can't read or write or do arithmetic or pay his bills. He is perfectly helpless, and you will simply have to do everything for him or he will get his affairs in a mess. There are however, two things he *can* do. Isn't that good? He can eat and he can cry. The latter he can do any time he wants, and he wants to rather often and at very odd times. The former is *very* tricky, and will be dealt with later. (That is, I will deal with it later. You'll have to deal with it right now. He's hungry again, and it is your baby.)

Keeping a baby requires a good deal of time, effort, thought and equipment, so unless you are prepared for this, we recommend that you start with a hamster, whose wants are far simpler. For a hamster, you need only a small cage, some cedar shavings, a bottle for water, and some seeds and tiny scraps of celery, lettuce, etc. If you are determined to try your hand at keeping a baby, you will need to provide yourself with a crib, a folding bath table (which you will never fold), and a carriage (you haven't got a car and *he* has to have his own carriage) to start off with, and later on you'll need a play pen, a table with a seat in the middle, a car seat and a car bed (and now you'll *have* to get a car). Still later you'll need kiddy kars, tricycles, bicycles, roller skates, ice skates, plaster casts, sutures, etc. You will need little knitted sheets, soft little blankets, little smooth towels and wash cloths, something mysteriously called a receiving blanket, and lots of puzzling little garments called gowns, wrappers, etc. Some babies also require caps and bootees, but these can often be obtained at little expense from an enthusiastic grandmother. However all babies require rubber sheeting and quilted crib pads and diapers. Diapers are a necessity, as they are used for diapering the baby, mopping the floor, making an impromptu apron (and from now on everything you do is going to be impromptu so you might as well get used to it), making a bottom sheet for the baby carriage, and spreading around on the crib in the vain hope that somehow if you spread enough diapers around on top of the sheets and pads and rubber sheeting and more pads it will all end up in less laundry.

The diaper, which is the most urgently needed article of apparel, is primarily a square or oblong of absorbent material which fits absolutely nothing. It is too small to be a sheet and too big to be a handkerchief. It is also too big to be a small baby's diaper and too small to be a big baby's diaper.

If you closely examine the shape of a diaper and the shape of a baby, you will find *no similarity whatsoever*. A person from another planet coming across a diaper for the first time would never in a million years guess its use.

Now for those who have never diapered a baby, here is how you do it. You spread out a clean diaper on a bed or table. Spread out a clean baby in his crib. Look at them both closely. Puzzling, isn't it? Fold the diaper sort of in thirds and then fold up one end

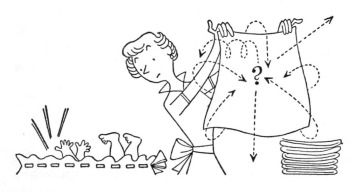

of the now-folded-in-thirds diaper about one third of the way. Put it on the baby quickly, pin it wherever you can without sticking yourself, and then hastily hide the whole, ill-fitting thing with some sort of gown or wrapper or receiving blanket. (So *that's* what a receiving blanket is for.) (I've always wondered.) (I thought maybe it was for dressing up to receive visitors.)

 REMEMBER ALL THIS TIME THAT THE HAMSTER NEEDS ONLY CEDAR SHAVINGS WHICH ARE CHANGED WEEKLY.

The one other absolute essential in keeping and attempting to raise a baby is a copy of Dr. Spock's *Baby and Child Care.* Do not attempt any baby-keeping at all until you have this book in your possession as it is *against the rules.* It might even be wise to obtain this book well ahead of time and study it with care *before* having the baby. Perhaps you will find, after careful and thoughtful examination of its contents that you would prefer to give up the whole idea after all.

A baby has no teeth, so unless you handle him very roughly, you need have no worries about biting. However presently, with considerable travail, teeth slowly appear. It is at this time that you must be on guard. Nevertheless, even before the teeth come in, it is wise not to handle the baby too roughly until he has become accustomed to you. Babies should not be picked up by an arm or a leg. You will notice, too, that babies do not have a fold of skin at the back of the neck, like kittens, and may not be picked up in this way by the mother's teeth. Babies should not be

[15]

picked up in such a way that their head hangs down, as their neck muscles are not strong enough to support the head. In fact, I'm not sure there is *any* way to pick up a baby. Maybe it would be best to let him lie there. Later, if you must move him, you could wrap him well in a blanket, and then lift him by the blanket. (So *that's* what a receiving blanket is for.)

There is no serious danger in keeping a baby during the first few months as he is quite unable to get about by himself. He can't even roll over. He will lie wherever you put him, and his only exercise consists in waving his arms and legs about. (Later he will send away for muscle building courses, but you needn't worry about that yet.)

Naturally you want to give him freedom to move his arms and legs, but at the same time, you want to avoid the possibility of drafts and colds. You therefore try to bundle him up tight in his gowns and wrappers and receiving blankets so he can't kick them off, yet loose enough to afford plenty of room for him to exercise. This poses a problem which causes new mothers considerable anxiety, and even induces hysteria and nervous breakdowns in some. Some mothers stay awake all night in order to cover up the baby every time he kicks his covers off, while others hermetically seal the entire house so that if he does kick the covers off, there will be no drafts. Still others wake their husbands up every hour and make *him* look to see if the baby is catching a cold. (He isn't, but the husband is.) Some buy special garments which are guaranteed to stay *on*—they are in effect a little sleeping bag—and then the mother stays up all night to make sure the baby doesn't get caught in it. (It is a curious fact, though, that these problems exist only for a first baby. Second babies, and all subsequent babies are allowed to kick off their covers and catch their colds in peace.) This dilemma lasts only until the baby is old enough to turn over by himself. By then, as it has become apparent that even a new mother cannot keep him covered, most mothers give up the struggle and go back to sleeping themselves.

When the baby is still extremely young, he is cleaned by oiling him up well with a piece of absorbent cotton and some baby oil. However this oiling is not customarily followed by a scraping, after the manner of the Romans, nor should he be beaten with birch twigs, like the Scandinavians. Just leave him as he is, all slippery and gooey. *He* won't mind.

But sooner or later, he is going to have to have a bath. In water. With soap. With a washcloth. In that folding tub you bought. That's what you bought it for. And this must somehow be accomplished without scalding him, freezing him, bruising him, drowning him, dropping him, breaking him, bumping him, frightening him, giving him pneumonia or getting soap in his eyes. However are you going to do it?

At this moment, if a grandmother, husband, sister-in-law or other callous intruder should arrive on the scene and laugh at your anxiety, pay no attention and go right on being as nervous as you like. The grandmother simply doesn't realize how fragile a baby is. Never mind that she bathed you. That's different. Besides, that was a long time ago, and it may have been sheer good luck that *you* didn't drown. Anyway, never mind how tough other babies are. This one isn't, and you must be extremely cautious.

HAMSTERS ARE VERY CLEAN LITTLE ANIMALS AND SHOULD NEVER BE BATHED.

When bathing a baby, there are two rules to remember. 1. Keep the baby's head above water at all times. 2. Be sure the pail is under the hose when emptying the bath. Failure to observe these rules is almost certain to result in trouble.

Most babies are fed about every three or four hours during the early weeks. Day *and* night. Night *and* day. Two o'clock in the morning for instance. Six o'clock in the morning too, for instance. And he can be very difficult about it. Sometimes the pediatrician says the baby needs to take five and a half ounces of milk and he'll only take four and a half. Then you have to stay up an extra hour or so, hoping that maybe he just has a bubble and then he'll take one more ounce. You have got to get that one ounce into him at all costs, or he will die of starvation, or get rickets. Coax him, urge him, beg him, and above all, pay no attention to your husband who is now standing around urging you to go back to bed and get some sleep. What does *he* know about babies?

If, after all your efforts, the baby absolutely refuses the rest of his milk, call the pediatrician. He'll be *glad* to chat with you at three o'clock in the morning. He was just sitting around with nothing to do anyway.

A HAMSTER IS FED DAILY. HIS FOOD IS PLACED IN HIS CAGE, AND HE CAN EAT IT WHENEVER HE FEELS LIKE IT. IT IS NOT NECESSARY TO WEIGH OR MEASURE IT.

[18]

A baby's things must be very clean, or he will get terrible germs. It is wise to boil everything he comes in contact with. The little bottle of water for him to drink, for instance, must be boiled constantly. You never know when he might want a drink of water, and water spoils rapidly, even when carefully re-frigerated. (Of course *how* you're going to know when he wants a drink of water is another question, as he can't talk. Still, a bottle of water is a good thing to keep around anyway to be one of the things you can try when he cries and you don't known why. He won't want the water of course, but it kills time.) Boil the baby's little vitamin droppers and spoons and rattles and stuffed animals. Boil his clothes and boil his diapers. Boil the little glass jars that hold his cotton swabs and safety pins. Boil his bootees and

caps. And when he's old enough to crawl around in the park and put all the gravel and grass in his mouth, you go right on boiling all his things at home. You wouldn't want him to be dirty, would you?

 THE HAMSTER'S WATER BOTTLE IS KEPT AT THE SIDE OF THE CAGE. IT IS CHANGED DAILY. IT IS NOT NECESSARY TO BOIL IT.

Presently, if the weather is fine and mild and the baby has obligingly gained some weight, the pediatrician will announce that you may now take him out for an airing in the carriage. However the pediatrician has no understanding of the problems involved. He has said you *may* take him out, but he has not explained when or how. After all, you can't jounce a baby around in a carriage too soon after he has eaten or he may "spit up." In a brand new infant, digestion is not always absolutely certain which direction it's going in, and "spitting up" is the euphemism describing the resulting confusion. Incidentally, baby raising is fraught with euphemisms like this which you might as well get used to. You can't wake him up from a sound sleep to put on his sweaters, and you can't take him out before his feeding time or he may get hungry on the way.

The question is not *may* he be taken out, but rather, *can* he be taken out? Perhaps it would be best to wait. It's a little cool today anyway, and the wind is coming from the East. After all, there is *oxygen* in the house, isn't there? Open a window, and wait a month or so. No need to rush things. He'll have plenty of time for going out later on. He has his whole life in front of him. If you start letting him go out now, what will he have to look forward to when he's eighteen? Next thing he'll be wanting to smoke.

 THE HAMSTER REMAINS IN HIS CAGE AT ALL TIMES AND REQUIRES NO OUT-DOOR AIRINGS.

Besides, if you do manage to get the baby out, how many sweaters should you put on him? First ask the baby's father. Then ask a grandmother or two. Then ask a couple of aunts. After you've had all their opinions, put on as many as you possibly can. First you put on one sweater because it feels a little chilly, and you would wear one sweater yourself. Then you put on one more because after all he's just going to be lying there and not moving around like you. Then you might put on one more because he's so little. Then you'd better put on just one more for luck. Then just as you're going out the door, you might put on one more for no reason at all, but just to be on the safe side. Now tuck him in carefully with a blanket. No, better put on two to keep his feet warm. Well, better safe than sorry, maybe you'd better put on a third.

Some new mothers call up the pediatrician and ask *him* how many sweaters the baby should wear, but this is foolish. *He* doesn't know how windy it is in your neighborhood. The best way is just to go out, tucking several extra sweaters and blankets in the foot of the carriage (along with a milk bottle, a water bottle, some vitamins—in case he develops anemia on the way—and a first aid kit, some diapers, some oil, some cotton swabs, some pins, a few extra crib pads, a couple of stuffed toys, a few milligrams of ascorbic acid and a freshly sterilized rattle) and then talk it over with all the mothers you meet outdoors. The first mother you meet with a young baby only has one sweater on hers. She is toughening him up. "You've got yours much too hot," she says. "He'll get all perspired, and then he'll catch a cold." She seems very authoritative about this, so you remove a few sweaters. The next mother you meet has six sweaters on her baby. "It's so chilly today," she says. "Aren't you afraid your baby will get pneumonia? He looks a little blue already."

By the time you get the baby's clothing and blankets adjusted to the proper warmth, it's time to go home and take them all off again anyway. And you can feel well satisfied with the outing. The baby has had *lots* of exercise.

 A HAMSTER REQUIRES NO CLOTHING OF ANY KIND.

TWO

On Your Mark, Get Set—

(including remarks on solid foods, walking, teething, toilet training, and other insurmountable obstacles)

In the beginning, all you have to cram into the baby is milk and vitamins, but one day the pediatrician will say, "Now you may start the baby on mashed banana." Or baby cereals. Or something mushy. Here again, it is easy enough for the pediatrician to say it. He doesn't have to come and get it into the baby. That's your department. Should you feed him the mashed banana *before* he drinks his milk, when he's very hungry and therefore more likely to try something new? Or, if he's very hungry will something other than milk make him very angry, and make him unable to take solid food as long as he lives? Or, if you give it to him after the milk, when he's feeling full, will he reject it because he's not hungry, and never in his entire life eat solid food? In fact, is it even possible to feed a baby anything but milk? This is a crucial moment. The baby cannot go through life living on milk. *The doctor has spoken.* You have got to get that food into him. Get on the phone again. Consult all of your relatives who have ever had babies. Go out again and consult all the other mothers in your neighborhood. Ask the elevator man on the way.

You will soon find that you are the *only one* who has any difficulty in the matter at all. The first mother you meet didn't give her baby *mashed banana. She* gave hers Pablum. What kind of a pediatrician do you have anyway? And there is no problem about when to give it. She gave hers the Pablum before the milk, and the baby didn't like it, but she got it into him anyway. "After all," she says, "the baby doesn't know what's good for him." The second mother didn't give hers solid food till he was six months old. What kind of a pediatrician do you have, anyway? And she gave it *after* the milk, and he loved it the very first time. The third mother gave hers strained liver when he was only four weeks old, and what kind of a pediatrician do you have anyway? She gave it in the *middle* of the feeding. It made him throw up, but after all, it's the *experience* that counts.

So you go home again, and you try it before the milk, during the milk, and after the milk. But yours doesn't like it any time. So you try cereal. He doesn't like that either.

Now a *problem* has developed. Here is this baby and he refuses to eat his solid food. ("Solid" in this case is a euphemism for "squushy.") Are you a failure as a parent? Is he a failure as a baby? Is the pediatrician a failure as a pediatrician? *Would* the baby rather have a hot pastrami sandwich?

This brings us to the primary rule of baby raising, which is the solution to this and all subsequent problems. This rule must be followed faithfully, and practiced regularly, and you should make it a habit to repeat it to yourself ten times a day. It is the *Golden Rule* of raising babies. *LIE*. Lie to your mother, lie to your sisters and aunts, and above all, lie to all the other mothers you meet on the street. When a newer mother than you asks for your help, tell her you never had the least trouble. *Your* baby just *loved* his mashed banana on the first try.

A crisis sometimes arises during the early months when you discover that Gesell's babies all hold up their right hand and look at it. Yours hasn't done this yet. The important thing now is not to mention this awful fact to your relatives and neighbors. Should any of them bring up the subject, remember the RULE. Meanwhile, call the pediatrician, never mind what time it is. However, he is often unsympathetic. Here you are with this baby that has something terrible the matter with it, and the pediatrician *doesn't care*. You can now find a new pediatrician who is less hard boiled, and you can also take the baby to a neurologist, an orthopedist and an ophthalmologist. Unfortunately, after you've made all the appointments, and told that first pediatrician just

[25]

what you think of him, the sly and traitorous baby will now, out of sheer contrariness, immediately hold up his right hand and look at it. I could tell he was a trouble maker from the start. As a matter of fact, he has been holding up his right hand and looking at it for weeks now, but he only did it while he was alone.

HAMSTERS DO NOT HAVE TO HOLD UP ONE PAW AT ANY SPECIFIC AGE.

The age at which a baby walks varies greatly with the individual, some managing it by a year while others may wait till they are eighteen months old. Some babies creep or crawl first at varying ages, some stand up first. I myself had a child who learned to sit when he was six months old and then never did another thing till he was eighteen months old. He never crawled, or crept, or stood up or moved around, and what's worse, he didn't even *care*. He sat there with his two parents standing over him imploring him to move around just a little bit, and he went right on playing with his little pegs and blocks and *laughed*. He didn't care that every other child in the park was galloping around pushing little push toys and pulling little pull toys. He just sat and smiled. After a time, we got into the hands of a capable neurologist who treated us with sedatives until the child got up and started pulling the lamps off all the tables. It was during this period that I was first working on THE RULE.

Of course for a time you can face this sort of situation out bravely by remarking from time to time that it's funny how a child will run around at home but just not want to move when he gets to the park. You can hint that these other babies are so *rough* that yours is a little afraid of them. You can point out that yours really talked terribly young. You can observe that these other babies get awfully *dirty* from playing in the gravel. But when the word finally gets out that that Smith baby hasn't *walked* yet, there's nothing for it but to go to another park for a while.

We then proceeded to have a second child who crept around at five months and was pulling the lamps off the tables by a year. However, in spite of all this activity he didn't walk till he was eighteen months old either. This absolutely proves my point, which, in the face of the entire medical profession I still believe to be true: LAMP TABLES SHOULD BE STEADIER.

Some babies have considerable trouble with teething. They may cry a lot and be fretful, and wake during the night for no apparent reason and in general make more fuss than you do for the extraction of an impacted lower third molar. The extraction of an impacted lower third molar, sometimes wittily called a wisdom tooth, is the most painful dental operation ever discovered. Whoever discovered it should have covered it right up again. So don't let the baby fool you. No matter how much he cries during the appearance of his first little incisors, they can't possibly hurt him all *that* much. He's just making a big fuss over nothing and acting like a *baby*. Sometimes, during this trying period a little paregoric, judiciously used, is helpful. If you drink a lot of it, it will help you to sleep through the baby's crying. Some people rub paregoric on the baby's gums, but after all, let's not be silly.

Teeth are supposed to come in in a certain order, but more often they appear in a state of terrible disorder. However, no matter how crooked the first set of teeth appears to be, you needn't worry about it. The second set will very likely be even crookeder, and you can start looking around for a reliable orthodontist, and this of course is the most painful part of the whole teething process as the pain is now all in the bank account which is the worst place.

The most important question that arises between the ages of one and two is, "Does he stay dry yet?" and the mother who cannot answer yes must go to the back of the park and study Spock and Gesell and fold diapers. No matter what happens from now on, she has lost caste and is not allowed to associate with the other mothers unless her baby should now prove his worth by suddenly doing something that no other baby has learned to do yet, such as memorizing the entire World Almanac or learning to ride his tricycle no-handed. It is therefore *necessary* to get *your* baby trained before any of the others so that you can be the one to ask the question first and feel the natural pride in your baby that is your right. After all, what did you get him for if not to be able to brag about him?

In trying to train a baby, the first step is to provide yourself with still another euphemism—a toidy seat. This object is intended to keep the baby from being alarmed and is actually designed for his own protection. However, immediately upon spotting it he becomes strongly suspicious. He thinks that someone is trying to civilize him and break his spirit. Your job, therefore, while strapping him firmly into the little seat with buckles and ropes and chains, is to convince him that you are totally disinterested in whether he ever becomes civilized or not. Don't let him see you kick the diaper pail. Evince utter nonchalance during the time he is sitting there. Hum, inspect your finger nails, bite a hangnail, pluck at the loose thread where your skirt is coming down, and when that ungrateful baby fails you utterly, there is always THE RULE to rely on. THE RULE will never fail you.

A canary or hamster or kitten or puppy may be returned to the pet store if it is found to be unsatisfactory in any way, and the pet store owner will be glad to exchange him for you. However, the hospital where you obtained the baby may be very uncooperative in this regard.

It is extremely noticeable during the first year or two of baby-raising that the house, which up till now you have thought of as a sort of home, has become increasingly filled with junk. There are folding bath tables in the bedrooms, play pens in the living room, high chairs in the kitchen, wash lines and drying racks everywhere, and baby carriages in the hallway. It's *discouraging*.

However, as the baby grows, you can gradually start to get rid of some of this acquired junk. He is outgrowing the baby carriage, the play pen and the bath table, and he will soon outgrow the crib and the high chair too. This is grand, really, because you can begin to have some hope of restoring your home to its original design. You can even begin to dream of the day when you can walk through a room without any particular athletic ability.

However, the baby carriage is soon replaced with a tricycle, the play pen with a desk, the high chair with a little table and chairs, the crib with a bed, etc., and in addition you now have a phonograph, a rocking horse, a swing hanging from a doorway, and any minute now you are going to find yourself with microscopes, punching bags, and a hamster in a cage on a bureau.

 THE HAMSTER REQUIRES NO SPECIAL TOYS OR FURNITURE. WHAT'S MORE, HE DOESN'T NEED A PET.

Worst of all, just as you were about to get rid of all that stuff and clear out the house, the next baby, or *sibling*, arrives, throwing the first baby into a perfect fury, throwing the house into a state of chaos, and throwing the parents into a state of shock, for they have now only two choices: to find a bigger place to live, or to sleep nestled on a couch in the living room with a bicycle and a play pen. The only member of the family who is now possibly better off than he was before is the new baby, and he doubts it.

Whatever experience the parents gained from the first baby, and it was plenty, can now come in handy, and make the raising of the second a snap, as they will know exactly what to do in each situation. At least they would if that foolish baby would only stick to the rules so carefully established by the first baby. You'd think he would. He has the same parents, the same crib, the same toys—but no. This one has to be an individual for some block-headed reason, and this one, while perfectly willing to eat his mashed banana, will not drink any milk.

For the next few years, utter chaos ensues. It not only ensues, it positively pursues, overtakes and finally outdistances you.

No two members of the family eat the same food

at the same time, no two get up or go to bed at the same time, and the only thing you can count on their all doing together is making more laundry than ever before. This brings us to the second rule, which is extremely important. Do not go on to the next lesson until you have thoroughly memorized this rule. Write it a hundred times, and say it over to yourself at odd moments while you're feeding the baby and putting all the books back in the bookcase for the fourteenth time because while you were feeding the baby, the older child, pitifully neglected, has suddenly become very literary. The rule is, *OH, WHAT'S THE USE?* Say it to yourself right now. There, doesn't that help a lot? Say it when the older child spills a whole glass of orange juice on his overalls for the third time that meal, say it when the baby rubs his spinach in his hair, say it when your husband comes home and says he's tired of hamburgers for the fourth night in a row, say it when the bath water all dumps itself on the floor because while you were bathing the baby the older one decided that little pail was just the thing to put his blocks in. Say it when a child steps on a graham cracker on the living room rug just as you put the carpet sweeper back in the closest, and say it every night, *with feeling,* just before you go to sleep. And when the baby wakes you a half hour later, it won't hurt a bit to say it again. *He* doesn't understand English anyway.

Important note: This book is intended for use only by parents having one child at a time. Parents with twins, triplets, quadruplets, quintuplets, etc. will have to get a book somewhere else. I told you at the *beginning* not to try more than one at first.

THREE

Table Manners

(including a frank and open discussion of ketchup)

Table manners are non-existent in infancy, and progress yearly to worse, worst and absolutely abominable. Of course you can't expect too much of a small baby. Table manners and etiquette are not inborn, and at the beginning you will simply have to wash the strained carrots out of his hair and ears for him, as he does not yet know how to use a napkin. Indeed, if you were to give him a napkin, he would probably just throw it on the floor anyway. Of course by the time he's nine or ten, you certainly give him a napkin to use, and he will not throw it on the floor. He will drop it on the floor.

Table manners are extremely important, as any adult member of a civilized society knows. We must all observe certain rules of conduct at table, or everything would be a complete and utter mess. And that is exactly what it is when there is a child at the table . . . a complete and utter mess dominated largely by ketchup. Indeed, one of the primary rules in breaking children to the table is to *keep all knowledge of ketchup from them as long as possible.* Ketchup is one of the most dangerous of all foods in consistency and color (as well as method of extraction from the bottle) with mustard, chocolate syrup and grape juice as runners-up. In the case of the first child, it is not so hard to keep him from learning about ketchup. He will not find out about it until he is old enough to visit another child's home for lunch. After that of course his eyes will be opened, and you can no longer hope to keep it from him. But in the case of succeeding children, the oldest child is likely to spill the beans, and you are then faced with the impossible situation of a child of two or three knowing about, and insisting on using, ketchup.

Other dangerous foods are potato chips (which break, fall on the floor and are promptly stepped on), peanuts (which leave mounds of shells and little brown papery skins on the floor), milk, plain or chocolate, (which leaves pools all over the place), and worst of all, the ice cream cone or ice cream sandwich or ice cream on a stick. These are all foods to be avoided until the child is twenty-two or twenty-three, and he should then eat them outside the home. One of the few real advantages of having an only child is the possibility of keeping him on a relatively safe diet of lamb chop and hamburger until he is old enough to handle the more dangerous items of food. Corn on the cob is another food strictly to be avoided as long as possible. I have seen corn cobs fly fifteen or twenty feet in the hands of a determined child,

striking a cat with considerable force at the end of the flight. Sometimes the flying cob may strike the glass and china on the table before reaching the cat, over-turning the cream pitcher and the ketchup bottle, and gathering considerable butter which then gets positively embedded in the cat's fur. And she is a desperately idiosyncratic animal who happens to detest butter in her fur.

As a matter of fact, there is *no* food which is not without certain hazards. A skillful child can get pretty good distance with a piece of roast beef or a particularly buttery bit of asparagus when he really tries. A good simple method of coping with these problems is to stick entirely to frankfurters without mustard and raw carrots, both of which can be firmly grasped in the hands and are neither drippy, gooey, brittle, crumbly, nor so heavy that should they strike the cat, or you, they would do any real damage. The frankfurter is a *bit* buttery, of course, and the roll a *bit* crumbly, but life has its sorrows and you cannot expect to raise children without some trouble.

 THE HAMSTER'S FOOD CONSISTS MAIN-LY IN SMALL DRIED SEEDS AND SMALL AMOUNTS OF RAW CARROT AND CELERY. HE DOES NOT EAT KETCHUP.

During the early years of childhood, the children eat alone in the kitchen, well shrouded in plastic aprons and bibs and helmets. The mother, too, is thoroughly hooded and gowned and shielded for the fray. But after a time the mother feels that it is time for the children to start to learn to eat properly, and to learn by example through watching the parents. Besides, she is good and sick and tired of fixing two sets of meals at two different times, and feels that it would be worth almost anything to be able to cook one meal for the whole family. Unfortunately, what happens is that the children's manners improve not one whit, as they now have access to more dangerous foods, and after a time, the parents' own manners deteriorate to the point where even they start knocking over milk glasses and mustard pots. The fact is that when you have said for the third quiet patient time, "Move your milk glass back from the edge of the table, dear," and nothing has happened, the quietness and patience are apt to dissolve into, "For Heaven's sake, *will* you move that glass?" And as you reach to do it yourself when there continues to be no response, there is a crash, and a splash, followed by a dash for a mop. For you have succeeded in knocking over not only the milk glass, but the sugar bowl, the cream pitcher (Limoges), a glass of tomato juice, and a little pannikin of melted butter, to the intense delight of the children who shriek merrily and resolve to knock over lots more things because it's such *fun*! See the sugar dissolving in the melted butter? See the milk running over the side of the table into Daddy's lap? See the tomato juice getting prettily marbleized with the cream and dripping into someone's shoe? What a good time everyone is having!

Of course as the children grow older, their fine coordination develops amazingly. They become capable of building tiny exquisitely fine model ships, preparing a section of a fly's wing for a microscope slide, winding the coil for an electromagnet, soldering neatly and cleanly, or making thirty yards of horse reins without dropping a stitch. Yet the minute they approach the breakfast table, shredded wheat is behind their ears, in the furthest reaches of the pot cupboards, in the cat's bed (and that same idiosyncratic cat doesn't like shredded wheat in her bed— I think you ought to get rid of that cat. She's a trouble maker). And the table is embellished with little heaps of sugar in a lake of milk. Pretty. "I couldn't help it," they say plaintively, should you venture to complain. "It was just an accident." Yet those same hands that are not capable of pouring milk from a pitcher into a bowl of cereal were only yesterday carefully and delicately hitching up the wires of a radio set without a slip.

Cutting meat with a knife and fork is a complex procedure, and only the foolish parent expects this accomplishment too young. These developmental strides take time, and the parent may well have gray hair, liver spots and a cracked voice before he has the pleasure of seeing his children cut their own meat properly. It is wisest to wait until the child is eighteen or twenty before demanding that he manage this manoeuver by himself. Until then, he may clutch the meat securely with the left hand, or foot if that proves easier for him, and saw away with the knife in his right hand until the meat flies across the room or you absolutely can't stand to watch the struggle any more and go to his assistance. Another excellent method is the one used by the Eskimos and some other primitive tribes. In this method, the child takes a bite of meat with whatever teeth are available to him at the time, and hangs on for dear life while hacking away the remaining portion close to the lips with a jackknife. This may not be good table manners in our culture, but it is excellent in Eskimo culture, and who are you to decide you're so superior? Note: Caution the child not to hack too close to his face. He is not old enough to shave yet anyway.

Some children early in life develop rigid likes and dislikes when it comes to food, and no matter how much you may explain to him that a well-brought-up child eats whatever is put in front of him, (and *enjoys* it, dammit) he will starve rather than touch a turnip. (And I can't say that I blame him, either.) He feels the same way about spinach, broccoli, carrots, asparagus, peas, string beans, lima beans, wax beans, rutabagas, Jerusalem artichokes, celeriac, beets, Brussels sprouts, cabbage, cauliflower, eggplant, mushrooms, parsnips, squash, and tomatoes. And he *hates* parsley. It will do no good whatever to tell him that some child in China or India would be glad to have it. He

will simply reply that he would be delighted to let the little child in India have it. Offering prizes for clean plates is of no avail. The only prizes that might work, you couldn't afford. And he will somehow get the perfectly crazy idea that eating parsnips is an unpleasant task to be done only for reward. Goodness. You could try forcing him to eat the parsnips by shoving it into him with brute force. But he might then get the perfectly crazy idea that he not only hates parsnips, but parents too. On the whole, probably the only thing to do is wait till he gets beri beri (which is imminent) and then say, "See? I told you so." Or, he may turn out to be immune to beri beri, and you may simply have to resign yourself to the awful fact that a malevolent fate has inflicted on you a child who will never, in his entire life, eat parsnips. Here you may well use Rule 2.

Some particularly sneaky little children like to make out that they don't eat anything at all, and get their parents perfectly frantic. They sit down at the table at meal times, and toy with their food until the parents turn blue with frustration. Alas, the parents don't know that this pathetic little creature, who has taken in not one single calorie nor fragment of vitamin, has just partaken of: two slices of bread liberally coated with peanut butter, three stalks of celery, a glass of chocolate milk, half a package of Spanish peanuts, two Hershey almond bars, most of a pound of cherries, three slices of bologna and half a package of Cheerios. Some time the next day, the mother will call the pediatrician, as she does regularly, to complain that her child *will not eat*, and she doesn't see how he can survive.

This is a hopeless situation. The mother will never find out the truth, because the child is no fool—he knows that if he tells what he ate, he'll be scolded for spoiling his appetite just before dinner. This whole family will go through life believing that this particular child lives on air. He weighs eighty-two pounds, but his mother is convinced that he is starving to death, and terribly fragile. Oh well. That's the way it goes sometimes.

FOUR

Discipline

(how to protect yourself from the child)

There are all kinds of parents. They are all, from their own point of view, perfectly wonderful, intelligent, understanding, self-sacrificing people. They are all, from their children's point of view, horrible monsters who are too strict, ignorant, old, ill-tempered and cruel. Some parents really are the one, some really are the other, and most fit somewhere in between. (I myself naturally fall into the first category, as I am always sweet tempered, helpful, loving, kind, tolerant, loyal, beautiful, a superb cook, elegantly groomed, soft-spoken, well mannered, and terribly good at algebra. In short, I am a perfect mother. Ask anyone.) (On second thought, just take my word for it.)

Among the vast majority of average parents, the mother is apt to be more indulgent than the father.

The father is traditionally the disciplinarian. When the child runs over the mailman with his tricycle, leaves the scene of the accident, shows little remorse (even though the mailman's shin is barked) and when finally tracked down, is just about to run over an old lady, the parents react differently.

"But he's so little," the mother says. "He didn't mean to do it. He's an angel really. He'd feel terrible if he really hurt anyone." (He wouldn't, actually.)

The father says, "He's a born criminal. He should be punished so he'll learn a lesson. He's headed straight for reform school. If you let him get away with this sort of thing now, he'll he holding up garages by the time he's twelve." (The father is right to object to the child holding up garages for two reasons: First because it is against the law in

most states, and second because there's far more money, really, in banks.)

This simply demonstrates that both parents are absolutely nutty. The truth is that the child is one of that vast number of perfectly mediocre children who are neither angels nor criminals. Very dull. He simply doesn't know how to steer very well, and what the parents should do is to let him practice steering in the family car till he's skillful enough to handle a tricycle safely. NOT ALL CHILDREN ARE EXPERT TRICYCLISTS. Perhaps this particular child's gifts lie in another direction. He might be better off taking up the study of classic languages for a while till his father cools off, and the mailman's shin heals.

 HAMSTERS DO NOT RIDE TRICYCLES.

Discipline is, in any case, a knotty problem for most parents. The question is, which acts require discipline, and what degree of punishment should be inflicted?

Spanking, hitting with old sneakers, throwing andirons, locking the child in a dungeon with nothing but bread and water for a week, slapping, pinching, biting, kicking, using stocks or the pillory are frowned upon by modern child psychologists. And by modern children, too. (Frowned upon for the parents, that is. These things are simply the signs of a healthy, out-going personality on the part of a child.) For one thing, it may give the child a feeling that someone is angry with him. And for another thing, he may hit back, and he is getting awfully strong.

Some modern parents solve these problems by sitting down quietly with the offending child, reasoning with him, explaining why his act was wrong, and then discussing with the child the suitable punishment. In this way the child is made to understand clearly just what he has done that is wrong, and as he has helped to decide on his own punishment, his resentment toward the parents is greatly lessened. However, this resolution of the problem, while possibly excellent for the child, is less so for the parents, who retire to their room with a blinding headache and an icebag.

Perhaps the best way to handle these problems as they come up is to react to the situation by flying off the handle, blowing your top, flipping your lid, baring your teeth, turning blue and screaming till exhausted. This leaves no doubt in anyone's mind that the parents are displeased by the child's little misdemeanor, including the neighbors for three blocks around. This method of dealing with infractions of rules has several advantages. By the time the parent is through screaming and is gradually regaining his natural color, he is in such a state of exhaustion that he is too limp to bother thinking up a punishment. The child (who has long since learned to ignore the screaming) thus gets off scot free. The parents are so conscience stricken at having overshot the mark (after all, all the child *did* was to start a neighborhood "Confidential" magazine) that they later apologize to the child, and buy him a new filter for his camera to make it up to him. *Everyone* is happy.

Of course far better than punishments is preventive discipline, in which you warn the child ahead of time that Mrs. Willoughby down the street is crotchety and doesn't like children riding their bikes through her rhododendrons. Suggest that they ride their bikes through Mrs. Hemingway's evergreens, as Mrs. Hemingway is away for the summer anyhow. This avoids later quarreling and punishments. Or, you might suggest to the children that if they make a slop in your kitchen just one more time, while mixing up their loathsome soft drinks and littering the place with sugar, paper cups, straws, lemon peels, etc., you will throw their new camera down the nearest cistern. DO NOT MAKE THREATS THAT YOU DO NOT INTEND TO CARRY OUT. This will undermine their confidence in you. Having once threatened to throw their camera down the cistern, if they do litter up the kitchen again (and they will, at three o'clock this afternoon when they come home from school) you *throw* their camera down the cistern.* *It's for their own good.* (Though it may not do the camera any good.) And for Heaven's sake, don't forget to tell them it hurts you more than it hurts them.

*If there is no cistern handy, use the nearest storm drain. If there is no storm drain handy, put the camera in the child's own bottom bureau drawer where it will disappear from view just as effectively.

FIVE

Cleanliness

(what is it? I've forgotten)

There are some children who are not always by instinct absolutely clean and neat. Some parents are distressed by this rakish, devil-may-care attitude on the part of their children, and wonder how in the world when they themselves are so extremely neat, their children have acquired such very untidy ways. They are further distressed when the accumulated rubbish and debris of the child's room overflows the bounds and comes billowing down the stairs and spreads out into the living room, the dining room, the kitchen, the back hall, the stair well, the front hall closet, the cellar, the front porch, the back porch, the father's den, the linen closet, the attic, the father's shop, the laundry, the parents' bedroom, all the bathrooms, and the front yard.

The parents of such children wish fervently that they could inculcate habits of neatness and cleanliness on them, but don't know just how to go about it.

These children have a peculiar ability to pick their way through mounds of rubbish, without squashing too many things, look bewilderedly about them, and say, "What mess? Where?" Or, equally, they may look down, puzzled, at a tee shirt stiff with paint and soft boiled egg and root beer, flick at it with a finger, and say, "Dirty? Where?" They may also look you straight in the eye, with a clear, frank, open countenance, and say, "Of course I brushed my teeth," with the evidence of the dry toothbrush not two feet away. They do sometimes, at gun point, wash their hands, but only the palms as far as the wrists. That is the rule. They will not go beyond the wrist, nor would they consider it playing the game to wash the backs of the hands. However, as few parents have a gun permit, most of these children never wash their hands at all.

Some of these children can be induced to take a bath by the threat of cutting off their allowance, or disconnecting the television set. When actually forced to sit in a tub of warm water, *some dirt does come off,* below the water level. If you want the top half to

get clean too, you'll just have to wait for summer and swimming, when a considerable amount of dirt will be removed from the top half as well, and even, occasionally, some from the back of the neck. However, unless the child does a lot of underwater swimming and surface diving, you can not hope to see much improvement behind the jaw and ears until he attends his first dance, at which time he may actually wash, with soap and water, all by himself.

The child's room is a sight to make strong men faint, and induces in mothers a condition characterized by trembling, pallor, dysphasia, weakness, hyperchlorhydria (which is associated with the ulcer that has just developed) and hyperbulia.*

The room is characterized by litter to a depth of two to three feet, except under the bed where it is perhaps only six inches deep. You can see no article of furniture, each being buried completely, and emerging as simply a higher mound of rubbish. You once, many years before, saw an occasional bureau top (let me see, was it maple?) or a desk top (birch— I *think*) but alas, they are only a memory now. A few bits of furniture stick up above the level of the rubbish—the very top of a desk lamp protrudes above a mountain of papers, books, crayons, hedge shears, gym sneakers (which he still insists were stolen from his locker in school), the remains of a tongue sandwich he made himself after school one day last week, two peach pits (not yet dry), a camera, a microscope, some jars of extremely aromatic pond water, a deck of marked cards (used for magic tricks

*Hyperbulia is actually a chronic condition afflicting parents. The main symptom is excessive eagerness for activity, resulting in ill considered action.

—you *hope*), coping saws, overdue library books, bicycle tire pumps, a Siamese fighting fish no longer in the prime of life who lives in the bottom half of a cider jug, and so on and so on and so on, right up to the top of the desk lamp. You look at the top of the lamp happily. "At last," you say, as you totter across the room, "a landmark!"

Some parents feel that this situation is entirely hopeless, and that they must simply resign themselves to living in a sea of clutter till the childen get married, or at least run away from home, or go to sea, or join the French Foreign Legion—there must be some way of getting rid of them.

Others attempt ineffectively to stem the mounting tide by periodically carting rubbish out of the house in grocery store boxes and crates. This is usually

futile, because the child stands by wailing piteously, "Don't throw *that* away—I *need* that." "That" happens to be a collection of peculiarly repulsive torn and sticky balloons for which he has some unimaginable (but intensely important) project in mind, like melting them down in your oven and creating something wonderful out of them. In fact, each loathsome object that you dare to touch turns out to be something really necessary. You can't throw those away—those are his bottles that he is going to fill with colored water. You can't throw that tattered old rag away—that's his favorite hand puppet. You can't throw out that beat-up old orange crate—that's his mouse house. You can't throw away that broken clock —he needs that for the gears and wheels. You can't throw away that tangle of wires—he needs those to build a motor. And so on and so on and so on, ad infinitum.

Sometimes a few small bits of torn paper or a broken crayon actually *is* removed from the child's room, whereupon the other child instantly pounces on it with glad cries, proclaims happily that it is *just what he has always wanted*, and drags it off, to add to his own collection. Often there may be a *complete interchange* of possessions, and sometimes for a moment or two while the exchange is going on and things are being stirred about, you may, for a moment or two, if you are alert and look *sharp*, find a tiny bit of floor to sweep. Of course if you don't move fast enough, it gets covered up again and the opportunity is gone for months—possibly for years.

Some mothers treat this problem by standing in the hall (which is as a matter of fact, the only place they can find *to* stand) and screaming. This method while giving remarkable relief to the mother, gives little relief to anyone else and fails utterly to result in any improvement in the children's rooms. Oh dear.

Another method which I have experimented with myself is to turn on the vacuum cleaner and first let it suck up anything that will fit in the nozzle. Then reverse it, stand back, and let it blow. Something always does result from this method, that I guarantee, but the result may be unpredictable.

My husband's method is one which you may wish to try for yourself. In this method, the parents prepare a little bundle on a stick, give each child fifty cents, and tell him he is now old enough to be on his own. Pack a toothbrush and a clean pair of socks and one clean set of underwear in his little bundle. He'd never dream of using them, but it's wise to put them in anyway, in case the SPCC decides to interfere. Should this fail, you can try leaving the children at home, and prepare a little bundle for yourself. However, in this case you'll need a great deal more than fifty cents.

When all else fails, there is one absolutely sure fire way of getting everything cleaned up at once. Put your house up for sale at a low price, and make it a condition of the sale that the purchaser *has* to take whatever he finds left behind. You may have to set the price low indeed, but think how good you'll feel. As soon as all the papers are signed and the deed transferred, you take one toothbrush for each member of the family, whatever cash you can find in the children's piggy banks, and you start life all over again, perhaps in another part of the country, or even in another part of the world, where there will be no chance for ugly memories to pursue you. This time, having learned your lesson, you will provide shelter from the rain and wind, fire for cooking, and one mattress apiece. You will steer clear of clothing, furniture, books, records, dishes, toys, typewriters, and all the other foolish, useless clutter of modern living.

SIX

Developing the Ingoing Personality

The average intelligent, thoughtful, careful, educated, loving parent wants his child to have a healthy, outgoing personality, and strives in every way to accomplish this, even going so far as to read the complete works of Gesell & Ilg, Spock, Levine, Freud, Reik, etc.

The only trouble with this endeavor is that it is *entirely wrong*. These misguided parents are *reading the wrong books*. The only really good book on the subject is this one.

Actually, a sickly, ingoing personality is far more desirable than a healthy, outgoing one, especially from the parents' point of view.

What really is meant by a healthy, outgoing well-rounded personality? It means that the child is going to clutter up the house with hordes of horrid little friends, all drinking Coca-Cola, stomping up and down the stairs, engaging in nefarious activities like wrestling and sliding down banisters, putting their grubby little hands on your new slip covers, playing phonographs, filling your kitchen with chemical equipment, screaming, slamming doors, and generally making life unbearable. Especially if you happen to have a headache. The child with a well-rounded personality is going to have to be supplied with books *and* baseball bats, microscopes *and* tennis rackets, paints *and* swim fins, records *and* pogo sticks, chemistry sets *and* bicycles, eyeglasses *and* ankle supports. Now consider a whole family of well-rounded, healthy, outgoing children. The mind boggles.

On the other hand, a child with a sickly, ingoing personality who isn't well-rounded at all, but merely well-focused on one particular interest, will come home quietly after school, with no friends at all, or at most one other quiet ingoing friend. He will quietly help himself to his Coke, go to his room, (with or without friend) and read till dinner time. The house is peaceful, quiet, ungrubby, and prosperous. For *this* child doesn't need the baseball bats, the swim fins, the pogo sticks, the roller skates, the bicycles. All he needs is to be taken to the public library once in a while, and he's happy.

What this country needs is more introverted children. We have a plethora right now of baseball players, and hearty physical types. You can hardly work your way through a small town or a suburban community for the baseball bats and playing fields,

while the library is a haven of peace and solitude. Children coming out of school at three o'clock are so covered with baseball caps, the mothers can't even tell which are their own children.

Teachers, PTAs, psychologists, psychiatrists, physical education instructors, and the parents themselves have somehow got the whole wrong goal, and they're all working like mad at it. There they are, bringing out all those children—the thought is frightening— when what they should be doing is pushing them back in. They're too far out right now.

I myself have always had a sickly ingoing personality developed to its fullest, married a man of the same high type, and am busily engaged in successfully raising two thoroughly introverted children, neither of whom can play baseball. Life *can* be beautiful.

If you are afflicted with the outgoing type of personality, before you know it you're engaged in club work, political work, PTA work, charitable work, and you're all worn out. Meanwhile your husband is out playing tennis like a mad thing in the hot sun, joining the Elks, playing poker with the boys, and is on the Town Council besides, and umpires baseball games in between. Everybody goes swimming and fishing and boating and golfing and getting sunburned and cross when they could all be lying down quietly at home, reading a good book.

Furthermore, the healthy, outgoing child is not afraid of anybody. He's not afraid of teachers, policemen, school principals, doctors, railroad conductors, audiences at school plays, and especially parents. He is perfectly willing to walk up to a perfect stranger and ask the time, or ask directions. *This is not normal.* Somebody is raising somebody wrong.

How do you help a child to achieve a sickly ingoing personality? This is something that is worked at gradually by the whole family, and you can't accomplish miracles overnight. Most often it is the parents themselves who must change their ways, as children learn more by example than by teaching. Active parents who go springing about on tennis courts, and dragging hordes of people home for drinks afterwards, or who go running around jumping over things and flinging balls and making their blood *circulate** are not going to be very successful at raising ingoing children. These people should practice going limp all over until they have lost some of their excess muscle tone. Then when Saturday comes around, and all the other people are running around organizing picnics and ball games and getting all sticky and red in the face, the ingoing family can

---

*Many people live under the misapprehension that blood is supposed to circulate briskly to all parts of the body. This is very exhausting, and leads to a condition called "Tired Blood."

stay comfortably at home, reading and playing a snappy game of chess.

If your child is unfortunately already an outgoing type, due to your having too assiduously read your Spock and Gesell, and having carelessly allowed him to grow up with his spirit untrammeled, it isn't too late to start now to correct this condition. When he brings friends home from school, tell them they may not stay to play, and caution them not to slam the door as they go out. It's a start. And the saving in Coca-Cola and Kool-Aid alone will get your taxes paid up before you know it.

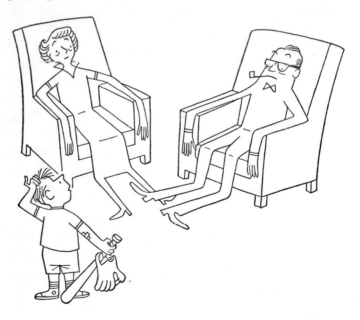

SEVEN

Family Fun

(including absolutely practical sure-fire suggestions for healthy, happy, wholesome, jolly, exhilarating, gay, cheery, invigorating, merry, and mirthful games for all the family)

Most parents realize the importance of healthy, happy wholesome family fun, in which all the members of the family take part. This helps to give the children a sense of *belonging*. I don't know what it gives the parents.

A great many parents would *like* to spend time with their children and play with them, but actually don't know how. Really there are many games for the whole family, in which every member can participate, even the smallest. As the sizes of families range from very small to utter madness, all my suggestions for games are carefully planned to be suitable for any number and for any ages.

A rainy Saturday or Sunday afternoon is the best

possible time for family fun, and here is a game you will all enjoy. It requires no equipment other than pencils, paper and a phonograph. Each member of the family sits on the floor, forming a circle. They then count off by twos, thus forming two teams. Just to make it more exciting, give the teams names, like the Tigers and the Bears, or the Lilies and the Azaleas. One of the children (and this is an excellent job for the littlest) may hand round paper and pencils. Another child then starts a record on the phonograph. Any good record will do, though Duke Ellington is a better choice. The parents have previously hidden in their pockets thirty-five cents per child. When the music starts, each player writes, as fast as he can, all the rivers of South America beginning with the letter Y. Allow about ninety seconds for this. Then the child tending the phonograph turns it off, and collects the papers and pencils, the parents distribute the thirty-five cents to each child and the parents choose to see which one drives the children down to the movie house for the Kiddie Matinee complete with chaperone. They're showing "The Monster From the Moon" and "The Horror From Outer Space" which should be a *good* double bill.

Another simple little game that the whole family will enjoy is one that we play often, as it requires no special equipment. It can be played at home or in the car equally well. In this game, the father offers a prize to the child who can maintain absolute silence for the longest period of time, and the prize increases with the length of time the game lasts. Some children become quite adept at this game, learning after some practice to keep silent for as much as ten or twelve minutes at a time without turning blue. While this game is being played, the parents offer up a silent prayer of gratitude for the little things that make life beautiful. This game is not only *grand fun* for everyone, but is truly educational as well, for if the prizes awarded to the winners are halfway decent, the children learn from practical experience that SILENCE IS TRULY GOLDEN. Sometimes caramels or jawbreakers judiciously offered just before the game starts can help to prolong the fun.

Another jolly little game that we all enjoy is called "Hide." This is similar to "Hide and Seek," but in "Hide" the children all run and find good hiding places. While they are hiding, the parents settle down comfortably in the living room and read the Sunday papers. This is a game that is full of merriment for all, as well as being wholesome and beneficial to the parents.

If all the children in the family are past eight, and capable of playing card games, a good game, full of fun and excitement for all, is a fast game of Black Jack, with real money instead of chips. The children can empty their piggy banks for this game, and often the parents can turn an enjoyable afternoon's fun into a quite profitable enterprise as well, especially as children are not quick to notice any little irregularities in dealing. They'll enjoy wearing little green eyeshades for this game, too. The secret here is to keep the game moving at a fast clip, with the stakes high. In this way the excitement is kept at a peak, and the children's rosy little faces and glittering eyes will be a *treat* for Daddy and Mommy. If the parents succeed in winning all the children's money (and this should be a cinch) it is only fair to give them each a

dime and let them run down to the ice cream store for a cone apiece. They will be delighted with your unexpected generosity.

In some families, reading aloud is considered one of the pleasant ways of passing time together, but it isn't. In the first place, books which are suitable for the children are not always suitable for adults (often inducing feelings of terror and nausea in the more sensitive parents), and in the second place, the reading of the younger children is apt to be halting, which leads to hair-tearing on the part of the father who has none too much of it anyway and should take better care of what remains. If the parents undertake the reading themselves to step up the pace from imperceptible to a bearable snail's, the interruptions may well lead to a severe case of hyperbulia on the part of one or both of the parents. The fact is that children are abysmally ignorant and their vocabularies distinctly limited. It is far better for them to go outdoors and get some fresh air until their command of English improves, and the parents can go back to reading their own books in peace. There is nothing more maddening than to have some illiterate little child keep asking silly questions like, "What is transcendental?" "What's syzygy?" "What were the Peloponnesian Wars?" "Who was Anaximander?" "What's a prefrontal lobotomy?" Such children are simply not ready for association with adult human beings. Get them a swing, and send them outside to swing on it.

A better way, really, for the whole family to have fun is for the parents to take their Black Jack winnings,* hire a sitter, choose some good television programs, leave a supply of frankfurters, peanuts and ice cream, kiss the children goodnight, and go out to dinner and the theater. Try it. You'll like it. You really will.

*Some people feel that these winnings should be applied to their 1959 taxes. I like to think of it as a nice little tax-free income, myself.

EIGHT

Health and Hygiene

(including a frank and open discussion of such subjects as stitches,
plaster casts, and the handling of unruly children who bleed)

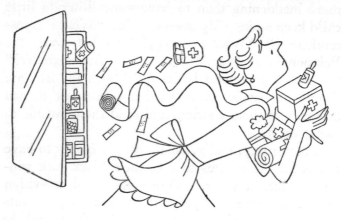

The minute a baby is born, certain health questions
arise and do not lie down again for a long time. It is
important for the mother to have an understanding
of the rules for maintaining health, and a knowledge
of how to handle the minor illnesses that occur that
should not require the services of a doctor.

The very first question in the mind of every new
mother (and every old mother too) is, How much
should a baby sleep? The answer is simple. A baby
should sleep as much as is humanly possible. What
else has he got to do? During the first few weeks he
should sleep all the time, just waking up long enough
to get enough milk into him to put him back to sleep
again. That answers how much a baby *should* sleep, if
he has any consideration whatever for his mother.

But, how much *does* a baby sleep? Unfortunately, the answer to this question is not simple, as the amount of sleep varies from baby to baby. The usual amount is not enough to give the mother enough sleep, or even time to finish folding the diapers and sterilizing things. If you are the fussy, old-fashioned type of person who considers sleep necessary, GIVE UP BABY RAISING AND GO BACK TO RAISING HAMSTERS.

When the baby is a little older, and no longer sleeps all the time between feedings, how many naps should he take? Well, he *should* take three. He should have a really nice long nap in the morning, and two decent ones in the afternoon. However, some babies get along with only two naps. Some get along with only one nap. Some get along with no naps at all. That is the kind of inconsiderate babies I raised. However, they got along beautifully. I didn't get along nearly so well.

 THE HAMSTER IS A NOCTURNAL ANIMAL AND SLEEPS NEARLY ALL DAY. HE DOESN'T DO MUCH AT NIGHT, EITHER.

Some children continue to take a nap after lunch even through kindergarten age, but this kind of luck is probably not given to just anyone. Very likely you have to be the kind of good person who actually cleans cellars to merit this kind of child. I tend to have dirty cellars and wakeful children on the whole. However, I did once clean the cellar some years ago, and although the children didn't nap, I couldn't help noticing that on that particular day every traffic light I came to (subsequent to cleaning the cellar) was green. (Unfortunately I have not been able to do further research on this subject as I have never again gotten around to cleaning the cellar. To tell you the truth, I really don't like to stand around in all that dust. So during the succeeding years, I have had to stop at traffic lights constantly, as it is against the law in my state to go through a red light. I only mention all this, as you might like to try this experiment for yourself. If you live in an apartment and the superintendent won't let you clean the cellar, try cleaning the closets or clean behind the stove, and see if it does any good.)

As the child grows older and passes the napping age, the next question of course is, how much sleep does a school age child require at night? Not wishing to be unscientific about this important question, I didn't depend on guesswork or my own limited experience. I went right to the children themselves, and asked about a hundred children of this age what time they went to bed. So, from the horse's mouth, I can answer that question exactly. The proper bedtime for a school age child is one o'clock in the morning. (Perhaps I ought to state, in the interest of scientific accuracy, that although I personally directed this research, the actual questioning was done by my children.)

The second most urgent question in the mind of the new mother is, How much should a baby eat? The answer to this is simple. He should eat as much as you can stuff into him, preferably more than any other baby in the neighborhood. If he doesn't, simply remember Rule One. As he grows older, the problem changes somewhat in character. He may go through the stages described in Chapter Two, during which

he may appear to eat nothing at all, but he will surely, sooner or later, go on to a third stage in which the problem is, How can we afford to go on feeding this monster? For he has suddenly turned into a bottomless maw which is constantly craving third and fourth helpings (mainly of the more expensive foods) with countless between meal meals. This is possibly the most trying time of all, as the food bills mount, and the mother is in a state of exhaustion from carrying home all that peanut butter. Here it may be well to offer a word of caution. Try not to have the child's tonsils taken out, as occasionally a child who previously was content to maintain life on an ordinary diet will, after the surgical removal of his tonsils and adenoids, start eating *as though food were a basic necessity of life.* I had two children who got along nicely while they had their tonsils and adenoids, but who, the minute these were removed, began eating like maniacs. The parents then didn't get along too well, although the supermarket where the mother shopped immediately leased the two adjacent stores and rebuilt into a grand new super-supermarket, and just the other day I saw the boss pull up in a new chauffeur-driven Cadillac. However, it is too late to do anything about it now, as *tonsils once out cannot be put back in*. Oh well. The parents meanwhile, have taken to eating less and less, and permanent worry lines have developed on their foreheads below the mother's graying hair and the father's receding hair.

And last, the new mother asks anxiously, How much weight should a baby gain? Here again, the answer is, as little as possible until he learns to walk, for of course as his weight goes up, yours goes down. Use Rule One when necessary. Remember that a too rapid gain in weight is not good for anybody, and in later childhood, it is to be assiduously avoided as the pair of dungarees you just bought this afternoon are too tight by tomorrow morning. This is economically unsound.

This brings us to Rule Three. RULE THREE. CHILDREN ARE ECONOMICALLY UNSOUND.

Another question frequently asked by mothers is, How can I tell whether my baby is right-handed or left-handed? A simple method of determining whether the baby is right or left handed is to watch him when he writes. If he writes with his left hand, you can be reasonably certain that he is left handed.

Can a child maintain optimal health on chocolate

and Coca-Cola? Yes. Again, upon questioning a fair sample of school age children, the concensus was that these are the only really *healthful* foods, and that they all felt just fine.

Should your child brush his baby teeth, or may he wait for the eruption of his permanent teeth to start toothbrushing? Actually this is a difficult question to answer, as I have never heard of *a case of true toothbrushing* occurring in childhood.

There are certain minor illnesses which the mother should be able to recognize and treat with little difficulty.

The most common is the head cold. If a child starts sneezing and his nose starts running, he may very likely have a cold in the head. On the other hand it might be the beginning of measles, chicken pox, mumps, whooping cough, German measles, roseola, or allergy to chicken feathers. As a matter of fact, there's really no telling what it might be. If at the end of a week he is all better, chances are it was only a head cold after all. However, if at the end of a week he is all covered with spots, it may turn out to be measles at that. In any case, the most perfectly scientific, medical, hygienic, sensible treatment is to put the offending child to bed and give him an aspirin and a pile of comic books. Keep in mind that comic books should be administered with caution, as they can sometimes lead to unexpected side effects such as drowsiness, nausea, etc., and may even, in some cases, have a deleterious effect on the brain when given in large doses at too frequent intervals. When in doubt, or at the first indications of any of these symptoms, change the treatment immediately to a dose of real, old-fashioned, hard cover books, which may be obtained without prescription at any good library.

In the event of stomach ache, nausea, pallor, fever, etc., the diagnosis is simple. He either ate something, or he's coming down with something, or it's a virus, or maybe it's appendicitis, or maybe he's taken an overdose of peanut butter, or maybe—well it could be almost anything. In the meantime, you can be perfectly safe in putting him to bed, and not giving him an aspirin till the doctor comes, and says it's either something he ate, or a virus, or he's coming down with something, etc., etc., etc. Actually it's hardly ever appendicitis, although during the twenties it was nearly always appendicitis.

He feels perfectly fine, but he is covered with red spots. In this case it's very likely poison ivy. Or maybe it's poison oak. Or poison sumac. Maybe it's chicken pox? Measles? German measles? An allergy to fish? Mosquito bites? What in the world is it? A person doesn't just break out in red spots for no reason at all, does he?

A bruise is easily recognized by a characteristic blackish-bluish mark on the skin. It is not necessary to put the child to bed.

A cut is easily recognized by a characteristic cut appearance of the skin. If it is also bleeding, you can be almost certain that a cut has taken place. Stick a band-aid on it.

When a particularly obstreperous child insists on getting a cut so large that a band-aid won't hold it together, the cut needs to be sewed up. This is usually done by a doctor as they have a corner on all the really good thread and needles, and anyway they use a different kind of stitch from any that we use. I have never known a doctor to use cross stitch, feather stitch or satin stitch, but I suppose as the stitches are all removed eventually, they take little pride in their work.

Among the members of my own family, (a quiet, peaceable lot) there seems to be some kind of contest to see who can get the most stitches, but I'm not sure who's supposed to give the prize. The cry that goes echoing through the house is, "How many stitches?" till an eavesdropper would think we were all making sweaters, and the fact is that not one of us can knit.

Before we had children, we used to buy black cars or tan cars, but after the children came we found these to be extremely impractical. We now have a bright red car. That way, on the trip to the hospital the people on the streets don't notice a thing, and the trip, already fraught with excitement is not made the

more hideous by the shrieks of passers-by. This helps to keep the children calm and avoids a public disturbance. Nobody likes to cause a public disturbance.

You can often tell when a bone is broken because it hurts, and this requires professional treatment too, as the average household does not have sufficient plaster around or any of those nice pieces of knitted stuff to put under the cast to keep it from being too itchy. A broken arm, leg, collarbone, etc., is actually far better than a head cold, if they absolutely must have something. (And they do. I have repeatedly told my children to cease immediately having head colds but they pay no attention. "Cease this instant," I say, but they go right on sneezing. It's discouraging.) However, while a cold in the head is simply a misery, a spanking new white plaster cast is a source of pride and joy and will give him a happy memory that will stay with him for years.

The doctor's bill, in this case, is not a source of pride and joy to the parents, who selfishly wish the child had never broken his arm in the first place. However, there is little use in taking safety measures around the house. "Come down off that garage roof this instant," you shout to a precariously balanced child, "before you break a leg or something." He comes down off the garage roof, intact, and that night he falls out of bed and breaks his collarbone. (That'll teach *you* to go spoiling his fun.) It is interesting to note here that husbands, too, though persuaded not to try to fix that loose roof shingle on the grounds that they will fall off the ladder and break something, will, the following day, trip over a crack in the sidewalk on the way to work and break several wrists or fingers. (Probably husbands are economically unsound, too.) (Besides, they have so damn many *ties*.) (And shoes.)

Many children get mumps, measles, chicken pox, etc. It is quite possible to live through these episodes. However, should the father come down with them too, my advice to the mother is to escape to some remote mountain region of South America and start life all over again.

NINE

Sibling Rivalry

(up-to-date instructions for playing this game,
including full rules for referees)

Sibling Rivalry is a condition that is rampant in middle and upper income families of the United States where it was invented by child psychologists. In the lowest income groups where it is not against the rules for the parents to slug it out with the children, it is less commonly found.

In a great many families, this condition is so severe that parents live in dread. It is considered to be worse than chicken pox, the black death, and snow in a television set.

At the very beginning of Sibling Rivalry, when it was first invented, people believed that the prevention or cure lay in cosseting the oldest child and presenting him with little gifts until he became accustomed to the baby. However when the baby then fell victim to the disease, it seemed that there was no cure possible and that Sibling Rivalry would have to be considered as inevitable as death and taxes. This, as it happens, is simply true. However I intend to show that the condition can be alleviated.

Many parents faced with this situation do not know how to cope with it correctly as they do not have sufficient understanding of the Basic Causes underlying this difficult emotional phenomenon.

In nearly all cases of Sibling Rivalry the main cause is *the birth of a second child*. Once having acquired an understanding of this underlying cause we can go on, if we keep our chin up and make a real effort.

The birth of the second baby causes feelings of antagonism and insecurity on the part of the first child, who expresses these feelings in direct physical form, thus causing feelings of antagonism and insecurity on the part of the second child, followed by feelings of antagonism and insecurity on the part of the parents. THE FAILURE OF THE PARENTS TO ACT ON THESE FEELINGS IS CALLED PARENTAL LOVE.

It is wise to prepare the first child ahead of time for the arrival of the second baby. (It may be wise for somebody to prepare the parents, too.) Plans should be carefully made so that the home life will not be too much altered by the second child, so the first child will not feel that the new baby is threatening his place in the family. This means of course that the new baby should refrain from crying and demanding attention while the older child is around, he should be made to understand that he ought not to get hungry and need feeding at a moment when the mother is busy playing a game with the older child, nor should he attempt to divert the mother's attention from the older child by such obvious methods as needing a diaper change.

There. That takes care of that. Now if someone will just think up a way to assure the *second* child that the *first* is not a threat, we'll be all set.

Should these methods fail, and Sibling Rivalry occur, there are steps that can be taken.

The first rule in Sibling Rivalry Control is to *separate the children at the first sign of any bleeding.* Secondly, *do not permit the use of firearms.* Third, *never let a round last more than six minutes.*

It is important that the parents show no favoritism. When the children have one of their little altercations, be fair. Listen carefully to the plaintiff and the defendant. Make it clear to the children that they must be calm and not raise their strident little voices. Only parents are allowed to scream. Insist

that they be ladies and gentlemen at all times. Do not permit the defendant to interrupt while the plaintiff is expressing his grievance, and vice versa. When each child has had a fair chance to tell his side of the story, and each has had a chance for a rebuttal and a summing up, and when the whole thing has become utterly incomprehensible (except that it all began because the defendant refused to allow the plaintiff the use of his woodburning tool, with which the plaintiff had intended to burn a beautiful design into the woodwork of his room—which is at present very ugly, being just plain, freshly-painted white—on the grounds that plaintiff had, only three weeks before, refused defendant use of his scissors with which he had intended to cut out some pretty designs on his plain green bedspread, and name-calling had ensued) you may throw back your head and howl. This helps to keep down blood pressure, which may have been rising rapidly.

After this, the best way to settle the problem justly is to go out the front door, slamming it behind you (so the wind won't blow it open again—if there's anything I can't bear it's a person who doesn't slam a door properly and forces somebody else to get up and go and close it again) and go buy a new hat, preferably expensive. Get one with lots of feathers on it—that's the best kind.

There. That'll teach those foolish children not to squabble.

Of course you must understand that a certain amount of little quarrels and tiffs is normal and natural. Remember that the children really love each other underneath it all. (All right, boys. Go to your corners. Round Two is over.) They really do.

The main thing is to make certain that each child

in the family feels secure in his parents' love. Yes, I love you Rosemary. I love you too, Billy. I love you, Ermentrude. I love you, Sam. I love you, Marguerite. I love you, Harry. I love you, Bettina. I love you, Arthur. I love you, Clarissa. I love you, Bertram. I love you, Dorothy. I love you, Carl. I love you, Elizabeth. I love you, Montmorency. I love you, Yvette. (Elizabeth, give Carl back his penknife, Carl, give Marguerite back her paper clip, Marguerite give Harry back his notebook, Harry give Billy back his toy truck, Billy give Yvette back her eyeglasses, Yvette give Montmorency back his baseball bat, Montmorency give Dorothy back her diamond bracelet, Dorothy give Bertram back his typewriter—don't *throw* it—Bertram give Rosemary back her shotgun, Rosemary give Arthur back his Siamese fighting fish, Arthur give Bettina back her socks, Bettina give Sam back his unabridged dictionary, Sam give Clarissa back her eyelash curler, Clarissa give Ermentrude back her snowshoe, Ermentrude give Elizabeth back her chignon. For Heaven's sake, brush it *off* first.) When each child is thus assured of his parents' love, the Sibling Rivalry disappears. (*Who* threw that candlestick at Montmorency?)

Sibling Rivalry does not always take the obvious form of quarreling over possessions and privileges. Sometimes it may be expressed in *attempts to gain the attention of the parents* by, for example, seeing who can be told the most number of times to pick his blasted napkin up off the blasted floor, or who can get the most stitches in his head, or who has the most cavities, or, most commonly, who can catch the most colds and it counts extra if the cold is accompanied by a fever. These pitifully obvious efforts to attract attention should be frowned upon as they benefit no one but the doctor and the dentist and they've already been to Europe.

Sometimes the older child torments the younger by refusing to answer questions, merely saying monotonously over and over, "Shakespeare never repeats, why should I?" or "If you don't know I won't tell you." This drives the younger child to a frenzy of frustration, the mother out of the house, and the cat under the bed. (Where she hopes to find, perhaps, a bit of chicken liver or a fragrant and succulent fish head. There's no *telling* what's under that bed.) I spent an entire childhood with an older sister so devoted to the sentence "Shakespeare never repeats, why should I?" that my entire personality became permanently warped and developed a decided starboard list.

A frequent cause of Sibling Rivalry is the fact that one child has straight hair and the other wavy hair. (Whomever could I be thinking of?) Or that one fortunate child gets to wear braces on his teeth while the other has to make out as best he can without a wire or rubber band to his name.

An even more frequent cause of trouble between children is the fact that, in some families, *the older children are somehow larger than the younger chil-*

dren. This causes feelings of inferiority and helplessness in the younger ones, not in the least alleviated by the older ones' being allowed to stay up later, ride their bikes further, get a bigger allowance and be in a higher grade at school. It may be of some help to reverse this usual situation *by having the smaller children in the family first.*

The most distressing of all forms of Sibling Rivalry, however, and the one against which parents should be always on guard, is the attack of *helpfulness* which sometimes strikes children during their bouts of rivalry. In this phase of the battle, they vie with each other to see who can attract the most attention and praise *by serving the parents' breakfast to them in bed.* The more children there are involved in this undertaking, the more dangerous is this aspect of the problem, as there are more cups of underdone coffee and plates of overdone toast being bandied about, while the likelihood of obtaining a napkin or a lump of sugar is in no way improved. For the object here is not so much to feed the parents as to demonstrate lovableness, and the demonstration is generally enhanced by leapings about on the bed and joyous shouts of "Isn't the toast just the way you like it?" and "I let the coffee stay in the top of the pot ten seconds, wasn't that right?" (Of *course* it was right, who doesn't love discolored hot water and a lump of charcoal for breakfast?) Coffee stains on the new blankets* are not considered in any way to detract from the final score.

*Any mention of new blankets is purely coincidental and is in no way intended to refer to any real blankets. Of course I don't really *need* new blankets—if I handle them *very gently*, they do sort of hold together almost everywhere except at the edges.

Sibling Rivalry is deepened and exaggerated by having children all of the same sex, by having children of opposite sexes, by spacing the children further apart, by spacing them closer together, by having fewer children, by having more children, or by giving one a red toothbrush and the other a blue toothbrush. It is important for parents to understand these factors, and to take them into consideration before making any move at all, unless it's to a larger house.

How to Survive a Birthday Party

It is often necessary, during the course of a child's development, for the parents to undergo severe birthday parties. These occur at intervals of about a year for each child.

The parents may prepare themselves for these upheavals for several months in advance by getting from the family doctor shots of Vitamin B_{12} and protective doses of antitetanus serum though I doubt that it will do any good. A better way to prepare would be to inherit large sums of money, and hire magicians, clowns, ponies, knife-throwers, acrobats, unicyclists, caterers, orchestras, bartenders and all the other little things that go into making a children's party a success.

Most people, not having large sums of money

available to them, must suffer the full blow by letting the children putter about with potatoes, blind-folds, straws, etc., until it is time to administer the food.

The average birthday party for about twelve children costs about twenty dollars, and as the child whose birthday it is gets about twenty dollars' worth of presents, everybody comes out even but the parents.

The most successful way to run a birthday party for very young children, those around four years old, is to encourage simple spontaneity. What this means, really, is that after one or two feeble attempts to get the children to stand still long enough to listen, the mother throws up her hands in despair and makes no further attempt to organize any kind of games. Unfortunately, this simple spontaneity is apt to be complex when all twelve of them choose the same toy to play with at the same moment. However, children of this age *enjoy* hitting each other on the head with wooden trains and trucks and the wise mother doesn't interfere. At the end of the party all the new birthday toys are broken, all the party favors have been stepped on, the candy has been ground into the living room carpet, and everybody goes home crying except the birthday child who stays home crying. The father is giving the mother a triple bromide.

At a later age, around six, group play is what makes the party go. This means that these children, older, more sophisticated, and capable of organizing themselves, no longer wander around aimlessly hitting each other on the head with the new toys, but are now organized into *teams* which hit each other on the head. However, these children are not yet ready for *competitive* games. The wise mother waits until they are about nine for that kind of activity. That is if she survives the seventh and the eighth. (I have never been able to get past the eighth myself, though I realize that some intrepid mothers do go on giving birthday parties year after year, long after that. These mothers, however, are those who simply do not learn from experience.)

The eighth birthday is, for some reason I cannot understand, by all odds the worst. A party for eight year olds requires considerable organization and planning, and it is wise to notify the police ahead of time of the exact time and date. Should the weather be fine, and the party be held outdoors, the sensible mother warns all neighbors to evacuate their houses during the time the party is going on. By eight years of age, the children's little muscles have hardened and their voices have attained a peak never to be surpassed. (This peak refers to volume only.) They exhibit great interest in games and can achieve considerable speed in galloping about the house or grounds in pursuit of treasure, candy, games and each other. Unfortunately this amazing speed is not accompanied by an equivalent development in dexterity in going around corners, tables, etc., with occasional unpleasant results. (These unpleasant results are to the furniture rather than the children, as children of this age have remarkably hard heads.) One way to insure a really successful party that the children will enjoy is to *permit* them to play saluji in the dining room with their hot dogs or hamburgers. In fact, you might just as well permit it, as they will do it anyway, over your dead body if need be. Remember that they have no particular interest in whether you are alive or dead anyway. At that moment you do, of course, your only wish being fervently for the latter.

Some mothers try showing movies, or having the children watch television during part of the party, in the hope of quieting them down for a few minutes while she cooks the frankfurters, but this false quieting down only results in even more spontaneous bursts of hilarity and excitement later while in the presence of the mustard or ketchup.

It is a curious fact that many mothers do survive these birthday parties, perhaps through some law of nature that gives them added strength during times of stress.

Desperate though it all sounds (sounds, nothing! —*is*) there are ways of alleviating the pain. Mind you, I don't pretend to be a miracle worker. I can't promise you painless birthdays. But I think I can safely guarantee that some of the sting can be taken out.

One friend of mine has neatly solved the problem by serving double Martinis to any parents who happen to show up. By coincidence a good many happen to show up at her children's parties. The children go off in one room, the parents go off in another and close both doors. In time the Martinis take effect and numbness sets in. During the period of numbness, the parents are able to endure the noise with little pain. The children have a grand, unfettered time, with no scolding or admonitions, and the parents have a happy little time too. When it's all over, everyone agrees that it has been a delightful party. Of course the cake may have been sliced just a tiny bit askew, and the candles may have been set in place just the teeniest bit crooked, but who cared? And no one even

noticed that there were eleven candles for a child just turned seven.

Another simple solution to a difficult problem is to institute a treasure hunt. This takes a little preparation ahead of time. Clues must be thought out and printed neatly on slips of paper. You may plan to have the children hunt in pairs, and you want to set out the clues carefully so the teams don't get bunched up anywhere. The clues should be simple enough for them to understand while at the same time giving them the impression that in figuring them out they arc being terribly clever. So far, you may think, this idea is nothing new. You've all had treasure hunts at your parties. But now comes the good part that will change your entire outlook, and have you *anticipating* the next birthday party. The clues should be leading the children further and further from the house, and the last clue, after five or six have been easily found, should lead them some distance further still *to a place that doesn't exist.* Have the clue suggest clearly a certain location and then describe a tree or landmark of some kind that isn't there.

While the treasure hunt is going on, sit down quietly in the living room and watch television. (There are some very good commercials, lately.) Or read a book. Have a cup of coffee, if you like. Ask a friend in.

After several hours, when the treasure hunt is over, and the children give up and come back, they'll be too tired for further activity, and anyway it will be time to give them their supper and send them home. Give them each a prize for having tried so hard. And make it a good prize, too. It was worth it, wasn't it?

If the children are a little older, you might suggest that they bring their motorcycles and black leather jackets, and send them off on a scavenger hunt. This will be a real challenge to their ingenuity. Have them bring back a cup of water from Niagara Falls, a rock from the Grand Canyon, a lock of hair from Marilyn Monroe's head, a piece of the sleeve of Lincoln's coat chipped off his statue in the Lincoln Memorial, a barber from a town in Wyoming, all the loose cash from a gas station in Seattle, Plymouth Rock, and two sailors from San Diego. Naturally the one who gets back first is the winner, but everyone will have *fun.*

I almost forgot the most important trick of all in having a successful birthday party. In sending out the invitations, don't fail to note that any parent who delivers a child too early, or calls for him too late, will be fined.

ELEVEN

Heredity
and Environment

(an absolutely scientific discussion, guaranteed to relieve
your mind of any further worry on these subjects)

We have all heard of *heredity* and *environment* and
the part they play in the formation of the child's
individual character and personality.

Heredity is an extremely complex subject, far too
technical for the average non-biological person to
understand. However, stated in its simplest form,
it is that when two brown-haired parents suddenly
give birth to a red-haired child, everybody has to
rack his brain to remember great-aunt Sarah on the
father's side and second-cousin Mildred on the
mother's side, both of whom were violently red-
haired, or people are going to think it's funny. Unfortunately, having now remembered great-aunt

Sarah's red hair, you may also now remember her terrible temper, her disagreeable habit of telling people exactly what she thought of them, and her susceptibility to hives, and wonder if this redheaded child you have just produced is going to inherit these tendencies along with the red hair. However, as second-cousin Mildred was an easy going type who slopped through life with her slip showing and got along wonderfully with everyone, it's hard to say.

When you consider that for every dominant factor showing in the parents (such as brown hair, curly hair, brown eyes, etc.) each parent might or might not also be carrying a recessive trait (blond hair, blue eyes, etc.) you can see that having a baby may be considered to be, at best, *a complete gamble*. When you further consider that in addition to the two parents, this baby also has four grandparents, eight great-grandparents, and so on, the possibilities are staggering.

 WHEN BUYING A HAMSTER OR A KITTEN, YOU MAY LOOK THEM OVER CAREFULLY, AND CHOOSE THE MOST ACTIVE AND ALERT ONE WITH THE PRETTIEST FUR, THE BRIGHTEST EYES, AND SO ON. [IT IS DIFFICULT TO LOOK OVER A BABY AHEAD OF TIME.]

Frequently, when two people marry, they are *complete strangers* to each other. (Actually this is a good thing as it often takes weeks or even months before they find out that the other member of the marriage never puts his cigarette stubs really out.) So it often happens that a surprised parent will find himself the possessor of a baby about whom his wife's family exclaim in amazement, "Why, he's the very image of Aunt Hannah!" and the puzzled father has never even heard of Aunt Hannah before. This can be disconcerting until his own family appears on the scene and joyfully announces that the baby actually looks comically like his paternal great-grandfather, which is even more puzzling as this particular great-grandfather had a full beard, and it's hard to say what he looked like. However, everyone is now happy except the baby who is hungry and cross and wishes everyone would go away. He doesn't even care who* he looks like.

*I would be glad to say "whom" but don't like to appear to be showing off. I would even be glad to say, "I should be glad, etc.," but everyone would then think I meant, "I ought to be." English is a difficult language at best, and every sentence has its pitfalls. We can only be grateful that we're not French.

The arrival of each subsequent baby is greeted by exclamations over his remarkable resemblance to or dissimilarity to all previous children of these same parents, and either way it is considered to be highly unusual. I was so unlike my older sister that all I ever heard, as a child, was, "She doesn't look *anything* like her sister, does she?" This I understood to be a disparagement of my *excessive* height, *straight brown* hair, *large* feet, *slitty* eyes, and so on. The very same people who were so astonished at this remarkable difference between us are now equally astonished by the strong resemblance of my own two children. "My!" they say in wonderment, "they certainly do look a lot *alike,* don't they! Why you can hardly tell them apart." (This is perfectly silly as one is half a head taller than the other and two years older.) I take these remarks to be a disparagement of my ability to produce highly individual children, though I do feel that my husband should bear part of the blame.

The instant that fertilization of the ovum has taken place, *heredity is all over the lot,* and everything from that point on is intensely irrevocable. That baby is going to be whatever has been allotted to him in the shuffling of the genes or chromosomes (I told you this was highly technical) and he's stuck with it. (Now take my hair, for instance. No, never mind.)

However, a lot can be done to help matters. As soon as the child is born, the parents should start a special savings account for the orthodontist and the analyst. *And never forget that a good hairdresser can work wonders.* (That is, for everyone but me. I've never found a good hairdresser that would accept the challenge of my hair. They're afraid I'll spoil their reputation.)

The hairdresser brings us to Environment.

Environment is far easier to understand than heredity. Once you understand exactly what heredity is, *environment is everything else*. That's you. Of course it's also the climate, the food, the boy on the next street who threw a rock at him, the death of a beloved turtle, his tonsil operation, your financial status (which is not too good—just let me see that tax form again for a minute, will you?) that mean teacher who made him finish his arithmetic homework, your refusal to let him take up glass-blowing as a hobby at the age of seven, and so on. But mostly it's you.

A lot of very smart people, like doctors, psychologists, geneticists, physiologists, biochemists, astrologers, numerologists and phrenologists have argued for years over the part played by environment in determining the personality of the child. Some of them would have us believe that a baby is a lump of clay to be moulded to our will. This puts parents in an awkward position. Awkward is not exactly the word. We parents are on the spot, and I'm going to get us off.

A simple scientific experiment will prove absolutely that heredity is far and away the most important factor, with environment running a poor second. Take a newborn baby. Look at him. No *really* look at him. There, you see what I mean? Born stubborn. And there isn't a thing you can do about it except dig your heels in for the struggle.

For the past twenty or thirty years, desperate parents have been driving themselves mad in a vain effort to change the leopard's spots. They took children who were happily gifted with athletic ability and tried to turn them into good spellers, and they took children with a gift for music and tried to make accomplished diving experts out of them. While Mrs. X is unhappily saying, "Oh if only Billy could play tennis as well as Jimmy," Mrs. Y is just as unhappily saying, "Oh if only Jimmy could read as well as Billy." Now if Mrs. X and Mrs. Y will just relax for a minute, I can make them both happy.

The latest scientific word on this whole miserable subject comes directly from the laboratory of the world's foremost expert—me. I have made an enormous and intensified study of this question, although unfortunately I was only able to acquire two children for my work due to circumstances beyond my control. (Let me see that checkbook. I could have sworn there was enough left for that oil burner repair bill.) The results of ten years of devoted slavery in my laboratory prove conclusively that *all good qualities in a child are the result of environment, while all the bad ones are the result of poor heredity on the side of the other parent.*

There. Now that lets all us parents off the hook, and we can all go back to sleeping at night.

TWELVE

Look Out!
Your I.Q. Is Falling!

It is a curiously unknown but readily observable fact that as the children grow up, the parents' I.Q.s go down. This is best stated in a simple mathematical law: The I.Q. of the parent is in inverse ratio to the square of the children's ages. Any natural law is a statement which most accurately describes an observed phenomenon. This law which I like to call Smith's Law of Reciprocal Stupidity in the Parent-Child Interrelationship describes the phenomenon noticed in every family in which the parent replies to the child's questions, "Huh? Whadja say?" This law is a direct contradiction to the previously stated belief on the part of psychologists that the Intelligence Quotient is a permanent indication of mental ability on the part of an individual, regardless of learning, education, age, or other changing factors. This error on the part of the intelligence testers was a naïve and wishful thought, due, no doubt, to insufficient testing. The parents were not available for testing as they were all home doing laundry, playing Monopoly with minors, feeding babies strained squash, etc., all of which can be very well done on an I.Q. of 60 to 80. The error is doubtless also due in part to the fact that the psychologists were parents themselves.

As the psychologists have failed to explore this phenomenon, I have had to go into the matter to a small degree myself, and I have come to the following inescapable conclusions. The parents' I.Q.s start plummeting on the day of the first baby's birth, and continue to plummet for years and years and years until suddenly one day they wake up, and there they are—middle aged, and with the mentality of a bright ape.

The parents do not notice the change at this time, as they are too busy. Fortunately the tasks at which they are engaged (opening and closing little stair gates, blowing up inflated toys, mixing flour and water, finding lost roller skate keys, cutting fingernails, doing jigsaw puzzles with four pieces missing, playing dot games and tick-tack-toe, picking up potato chips from the floor, etc.) do not require their former high intelligence, so from the practical standpoint the situation is not yet difficult. And as they are likely to associate mainly with other parents in the same condition, the low state of their I.Q. continues to go unnoticed. It is when the children get to the fourth and fifth grades, about, that they first begin to notice that something is wrong.

The discovery is first made when a child comes

home from school and demands help in dividing four hundred and eighty-seven by ninety-two. How in the world can this be accomplished? Ninety-two clearly won't go into forty-eight, and there isn't a zero in sight to help out. *Somewhere a cog has slipped.* You can solve the problem for a while by explaining that you're busy helping his younger brother with his horse reins (which he intends to sew into a little coat one of these days when he gets through making two hundred plaster spaniel dogs that he is making with a mold he has, which he will paint nicely and sell for five cents apiece, which will net him hundreds and hundreds of dollars with which he can buy more wool for longer and longer horse reins, until someday he will have horse reins that reach all the way around the block) or that you're busy helping the baby who is having trouble nesting six plastic hollow blocks (and it's *hard*). But it won't help for very long, because soon he comes home again and wants help in multiplying three-eighths by seven-ninths. You console yourself by telling yourself that this is perfectly silly as no one is ever, in real life, going to have to multiply three-eighths by seven-ninths. In fact, all the arithmetic you've needed to know for years and years now, is how to subtract a hundred and forty-one dollars from four hundred and twelve dollars, and even that isn't hard as all you have to do is write out the check and the bank will be glad to do the arithmetic for you on an adding machine, deducting an additional sum because your balance is now too low for the number of transactions you have made. (The reason the teller does this on an adding machine is that he is a parent too.) Sometimes you subtract four hundred and twelve dollars from a hundred and forty-one, and then the bank will do the arithmetic even faster for you. You'll hear from them before the ink is dry on the check. *The bank is your friend.* Nevertheless, the discovery that you cannot do this simple arithmetical multiplication is disquieting, as you are perfectly certain that you once were able to do it. *Another cog has slipped.*

Oh well, it's only arithmetic.

Then one day a sweet little voice says, "Mommy, what is a participial clause?" and all you can say is, "Huh?" Or, "What were the events leading to the War of 1812?" and you say, "Well, uh." Or, "What is the real significance of the Jones-Robinson Act of 1922?"* At this point you are faced with the in-

*It is my belief that I just made up this name and date, but my mind has slipped so far that for all I know, there may really *be* such an act. If there is, I wonder what its significance was?

eluctable realization that you really don't know a damned thing, and it might be better for the world at large if you were to give up voluntarily your rights as a citizen and cease voting.

Was Major Andre one of the good guys or one of the bad guys?

Who was Metternich?

How do you extract a square root?

What was the Monroe Doctrine?

What is a monocotyledon, and which part of a carrot is the cortex?

Is Australia a big island or a small continent?

What became of the Ottoman Empire?

What became of the Holy Roman Empire, if it comes to that?

How many rods to a mile, and how many pecks to a bushel?

Do you think I should go on the $64,000 question?

All this time those children are sopping up foolish information. They're learning to figure out if one pound of peaches costs twenty-nine cents, how much will a pound and a half cost. (There's really no need for this. The man in the supermarket will write it on the paper bag for you.) They are figuring out things like how far a fly will go if he keeps flying back and forth the length of a freight train that is going from New York to Buffalo at sixty miles an hour. They are learning to mispronounce words like Himalaya. (They say Him-a-*lay*-a, when everyone *knows* it should be Him-*ahl*-yuh.)

You may find it helpful to mislay your eyeglasses frequently.

Remind them that you are the only member of the family who knows the recipe for brownies.

[96]

Tell them that you really know the answer, but for their own good you would prefer that they look it up for themselves. Explain to them the importance of learning to use reference books and libraries.

When all else fails, keep reminding them that although your algebra may be a trifle rusty, and your French verbs have momentarily forsaken you (though they'll surely be right back at any moment now), and your European History is just a little weak, and you've sort of forgotten the main points of American History (let me see now, whose side were the Monitor and Merrimac on?) and your Latin has kind of gone, and your Ancient History never was much to start with, and your chemistry has just not been in use lately (though it's all just on the tip of your tongue and any minute now you'll be able to come up with the formula for water) still, THEY HAVEN'T YET ACQUIRED ANY WISDOM. You simply have to keep plugging away at this. Remind them of it constantly. Point out to them daily that you are older than they are and *you have learned a great deal that isn't in textbooks.**

*If they start asking "What?" don't answer.

THIRTEEN

Money Is the Root of All Children

Most people believe it is important to help children to develop a sense of responsibility in the early years so that later on, as adult men and women, they may become good citizens and useful members of society. A sense of responsibility can be developed even in younger children. It has to be, because otherwise he will come home from school, having lost one of his shoes, and upon having his attention called to this slight disorder in his dress, he will say carelessly, "It was Susie's fault." He threw his shoe at Susie, and Susie refused to pick it up and return it. (Susie has no sense of responsibility either.) When last seen, the shoe was being taken home by a beagle who lives in quite another part of town. (The beagle is the only one so far with any sense of responsibility. At least he knew better than to leave a perfectly good shoe lying around on a playground where someone could easily trip over it and fall, or where, at the very least, it would look untidy. And we all want to keep our playground clean, don't we?)

In order to develop this sense of responsibility the child needs to have a feeling of importance, a feeling that trust is being placed in him. (Of course he should only have a *feeling* that trust is being placed in him. You don't want to carry this character-building too far, or there won't be a shoe left in the house.)

One way to help to child develop reliability and responsibility is to establish an allowance which he must learn to spend in a sensible way on his own needs.

The weekly allowance is pretty much a universal custom, but the big question is, "How much?" Of course this depends greatly on the age of the child, the number of children in the family, and the economic status of the father. (Which is not good. Just let me see that bank statement again for a minute, will you?) It also depends greatly on how much Peggy gets. (It doesn't matter who Peggy is. Peggy is the mythical character brought into every family discussion. Peggy gets twenty dollars a week for spending money. Peggy is allowed to stay up to watch the Late Show every week. Peggy goes to the movies all the time. Peggy has chocolate milk for breakfast. Peggy's mother lets her have supper in the television room. Peggy can't read. Peggy smokes cigarettes whenever she feels like it. Peggy drinks coffee. Peggy is seven years old.) However in the puzzling question of how much allowance to give, there are two simple rules by which you can guide yourself. The first is to keep close to the standard established by the other families in your neighborhood. The second is to give what you think is the proper amount regardless of what the other families in your neighborhood do. If you keep these two rules clearly in mind at all times, you can't go wrong. You *can* go crazy.

THE HAMSTER IS NEVER GIVEN AN ALLOWANCE AS HE SIMPLY STORES IT IN HIS POUCHES AND THE MONEY IS THEN PERMANENTLY OUT OF CIRCULATION WHICH IS NOT GOOD FOR THE ECONOMY OF THE COUNTRY. IT IS NOT PARTICULARLY GOOD FOR THE HAMSTER EITHER.

After all, remember that in the matter of allowances, the amount of money is not important. It is the idea that this money is entrusted to the child to spend as he sees fit. It helps him to learn the importance of spending wisely, the importance of saving, and the impossibility of buying a good camera.

When the allowance is decided upon, the parents must discuss with the child just what he is expected to pay for with this money. Is it purely spending money, or must he also pay for his own school supplies, cigarettes, camera film, etc.? Let us take, for example, a child whose allowance is twenty-five cents a week. Should he simply squander this money on toys, games, microscopes, tricks, crayons, stamps, ice cream cones, encyclopedias and other foolish things? Or should he pay for the lost shoe? (Should Susie pay for the lost shoe? Should the beagle pay for the lost shoe?) If this child is allowed to grow up without paying for that shoe, he may go through life losing shoes without ever feeling responsible for them. On the other hand, at twenty-five cents a week, he will be without shoes for quite a while, and the neighbors may think it's funny. What do *they* care about his character? So maybe just this once it would be best to raise his allowance to eight ninety-five, and go back to twenty-five cents next week.

It is important for the parents to maintain their hold on reality at this time, and to put out of their minds all memories of five cent ice cream cones, five cent jelly apples, five cent candy bars, five cent magazines, five cent subway fares, five cent telephone calls, and five cent cigars. It is also important for the parents to put out of their minds all thoughts of savings accounts, winter coats and other fripperies of their youth. It is simply not realistic to expect a child these days to take care of all his needs, clothes, carfares, lunches, spending money, etc., on an allowance of a quarter a week. If you expect all that, you will have to raise him to fifty cents.

Of course children do have other sources of income. They often collect quite a bit at birthdays and Christmas from out of town relatives, a few find jobs to do around the neighborhood, and they all have a fairly steady source of income from the loss of teeth, which sometimes seem to come out in handfuls. This brings us to Rule Four: ALWAYS REMOVE THE TOOTH FROM UNDER THE PILLOW WHEN PUTTING THE MONEY THERE, TO ELIMINATE THE POSSIBILITY OF TOOTH-HOARDING. Otherwise the same tooth may be used over and over, till the whole family ends in utter financial ruin, while that one particular child

is wallowing in cameras, generators, telescopes, etc. It is not good for him to have so many things. It is wise, too, to insist on seeing the space in the mouth before forking over the cash. One of our children recently mailed us several teeth from camp, with a demand for cash to be remitted at once. While I do not deny the possibility that some of these teeth are legitimately his, one in particular does not look absolutely like a human tooth. Rule Four is probably one of the most important rules in child-raising.

 THE HAMSTER'S TEETH ARE EXTREMELY SHARP. BUT AT LEAST THEY DON'T FALL OUT. THIS IS A GOOD THING, AS HE HAS NO PILLOW ANYWAY.

Some children find a good source of earnings in taking pictures of the neighbors' houses and gardens and children, in putting out a neighborhood newspaper, in entertaining at children's parties, etc. Sometimes the amounts amassed by an enterprising child can run up to as much as two or three dollars. This is a particularly good time to help the child develop a sense of responsibility and belonging to the family. Are you going to let him get away with spending all that money on himself? Do you want him to grow up to be selfish? How about spending a pleasant Saturday at home as outlined in Chapter VI?

There. That'll build his character. And it will spread the loot around a little, too.

FOURTEEN

Infinite Kittens in a Little Room

Another way of developing responsibility is by giving the child his very own pet. You can start him out with a goldfish or a turtle. This will require simply that he put a little food in the tank once in a while. As a matter of fact, the oftener he forgets, the better off the fish or turtle is because he always gives them too much food anyway. But the best thing of all is that neither of these pets lives very long anyhow, and you can quickly get rid of the whole mess. Which you might just as well do, because they weren't any fun anyway. You can't hug a fish.

After the fish or turtle, you might try some kind of viviparous tropical fish. They're exciting and educational, too, as the child can really watch the life cycle before his very eyes. Oh dear, was he at school when she gave birth? And she's eaten all the babies? That is too bad, isn't it. Well, let's get on to the

Parakeet. The parakeet is really *fun*. You can train it to sit on your finger, and then you can teach it to talk, and let it fly around the house and perch on your head. At least, the man in the store said it would. And it will be much better for developing responsibility, as the bird will require food, water, gravel, cuttle-bone, and a thorough cage-cleaning every day. You simply have to have a little patience, and put your hand in the cage, gently put your finger against the bird's legs, and repeat his name softly but clearly over and over. Here, Petie, Petie, Petie, here Petie, Petie. Nice Petie. Come on, Petie. Good Petie. Here, Petie, Petie, Petie. Come on Petie. Come *on*, Petie. Come *on* I say. *Will* you get on my finger? Dammit, I said perch on my finger, you stupid bird.

It is not hard to get rid of a parakeet. Lots of neighbors will take him gladly for their children, especially after you explain how to train him and make a loving adorable pet of him. Oh well. On to

The hamster. The hamster is a lovable little ball of golden fur. He requires little care (which is fortunate as that is what he gets). He resides in a small cage and is fed bits of carrot, celery, lettuce, fruit, also any kind of seeds or nuts, bread and occasional tiny scraps of meat. He needs cedar shavings for the bottom of his cage, and he is extremely neat and clean in his habits. His cage is cleaned weekly, and of course, like all animals, he must have fresh water to drink every day. He is easily tamed, and within a day or so will come out of his cage and sit on your hand and eat the seeds you hold in your palm. He is a bright, alert little creature, and everyone in the family will take to him right away. Isn't he cute? You'd never think he was really just a kind of rat, would you? See how he sits up and looks at you when you call him? Isn't he a *smart* little thing? You'd almost think he *understood* you. (Have you given him his water today, dear? You forgot. But you'll remember tomorrow. How many days is it since you last gave him fresh water? You think about a week or two. Have you given him a carrot, sweetheart? When? You think you remembered last November?) The hamster is a darling pet, and is very good for developing character—in the mother. She will learn restraint and self-control as well as responsibility.

That nice lady around the corner with five children will be *glad* to have the hamster. One of her children *said* so, didn't he? Well take it over there. Quick. And let's get a

Kitten. Now a kitten really is a *pet*. You can pick a kitten up and hold her and love her. She is so soft and cuddly and warm, and what a *pretty face* she has. Oh dear! She hasn't learned to sheath her claws yet, has she. Don't just stand there, darling, you're dripping blood on the new rug. Run in the bathroom, dear, linoleum is so much easier to wipe off. Here darling, let mommy mop you up. Never mind. Kitty will grow up into a lovely soft gentle cat very soon. Besides a kitten is terribly easy to train. All she needs is a box or pan with some shredded newspaper or sand in it. She really wants to be clean, you see, so she'll only use a place where she can hide everything. Isn't that *good*? The sofa cushions? Why should I look under the sofa cushions? Why that adorable little bundle of fur has found another place, hasn't she. Wasn't she clever? She really did hide it. Well, perhaps Daddy will buy us all a new sofa after all. Anyway, it doesn't matter. She is so cute! Couldn't you just eat her up? See how she pounces on the lamp cords? Isn't that darling? Oh well, before you know it, she'll be a full grown cat, and she'll outgrow all these little kitten ways. There, see, didn't I tell you she'd be full grown before you knew it? Aren't they the cutest things? Five! Well! Cute! I wonder if the milkman—no, he has six children and two dogs. How about the Schroeders? No. Their children are allergic. How about the—no. They have their own cats. How about an ad in the paper? A sign on the porch? Ask around in school. Ask anybody walking by on the street. See if the gardener . . . How about your cousins? Try the butcher. Did you *ask* the Milfords? I wonder if they wouldn't be good favors at our next birthday party? No, that's no good. The mothers would bring them back. I wonder if they'd get lost if we let them outside for some nice sunshine and fresh air? No. Their mother brings them back. Well don't just *stand* there. We have to do *something*. I know! Let's get a

Puppy. They're really not too expensive you know. After all, it doesn't have to be a show dog. And let's face it. A dog is really the only kind of pet to have. A dog *loves* you. You can teach him tricks. You can teach him to bark when burglars come, or to wake you up if the house catches fire. (Now if we could only teach him not to bark every time he sees a bird, cat, dog, car, bicycle, fly, or human being.) He will learn to bring in the morning paper for you. (And I do love a slobbered up paper with my coffee, don't

[107]

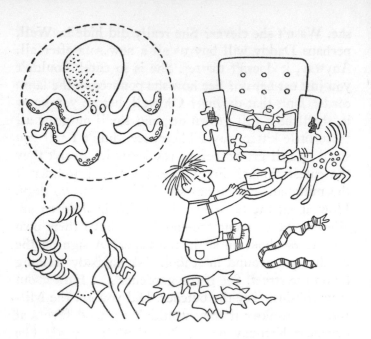

you?) You can teach him to sit up and beg, or shake hands, or roll over or lie down. (Now if you can only teach him not to chew hats . . .) You can take him out for a walk. You'd better take him out for a walk. Well it's your turn, I did it last night. Nobody remembered early this morning. He went by himself in the cellar. I don't care if you do have to practice the piano, you can do that later. You're the one who wanted a dog, you know. *I* certainly didn't want him. What do I need a dog for? I have children, haven't I? Well somebody has to do it. Now come on, which one of you children is it going to . . . oh. It's too late. Perhaps Daddy will buy us a new living room rug to go with the new sofa.

During the pet period the parents should at all times keep in mind Rule One, Rule Two, Rule Three and Rule Four, and any other rules they can think up that might help, such as A SOFT ANSWER TURNETH AWAY WRATH, A FOOL AND HIS MONEY ARE SOON PARTED, A BIRD IN THE HAND IS UNLIKELY, etc.

FIFTEEN

Never Send a Boy to Do a Boy's Job

Every child should take his share of the family's work around the house and grounds. In this way he learns to share responsibilities with the other members of the family unit, and to understand that to have a place in a social unit imposes obligations as well as conferring benefits. Then when he is grown up he will realize that when he sends his children to school, he must also join the PTA.

There are many jobs that even the smallest children can do, such as emptying waste baskets and ash trays, watering plants, feeding pets, and then later they can advance to helping to make the beds, raking leaves, shovelling snow, washing windows, watering the lawn, raking the gravel in the driveway, and so on. Any child can certainly help with setting the table and clearing away, as well as washing and drying dishes.

That is, they *can*—the only trouble is, they *won't*. Which is just as well, because if they *do* you wish they *didn't*.

They mean to of course. They really *want* to rake the driveway. In fact they're absolutely dying to rake the driveway. There isn't one thing in this world they'd rather do than rake the driveway. Why they'd rather rake that driveway than go to the frozen custard stand for a triple dip Martian Special De Luxe. The only trouble is that just this minute they're excruciatingly busy digging a moat in the back yard and filling it with water. And when they get through with that, they have to write out ten words for spelling, collect three pretty autumn leaves, and find samples of five different kinds of cloth for homework, and even a mother has to understand that homework comes first.

Of course children really enjoy having jobs to do. It's just that these particular jobs are not worthy of their enormous capabilities, their muscles of steel, their vast initiative, skill and experience. What they'd really like to do is paint and paper the whole house, take over all the driving, build an entire room full of book shelves, pave the whole driveway with concrete all by themselves, cook the whole dinner, and repaint the car. One row of radishes is too much trouble, but what they'd really like is to plant a half-acre of corn. Meanwhile they're far too busy and too tired to carry one waste basket downstairs for you.

You hold a family council, and you all agree that the children aren't babies any more and that they're old enough now to help and to take on a real responsibility. Everyone decides on his particular job, and all is harmony and joy.

"I'll do it every day," he says. "Don't you give it another thought. I'll attend to it, and you won't have to remind me."

Then Monday comes and Monday goes, and Tuesday comes and Tuesday goes. By Friday you decide it's time to mention it. (It's not that you mind leaves on the lawn, but you've been cut off from civilization for three days now. The mailman, milkman, oil truck driver and grocery store delivery man have decided not to risk it.) (This is sensible of them. The cat has been lost for two days too.) The following Monday you mention it again. "Gee, I'm sorry," he says with feeling, "I meant to, but I'll do it right now." Ten minutes later you find him lying on the floor of his room reading (without his eyeglasses and in the gathering dusk). Now you have two choices. You can demand that he get up and do it right this minute, or you can say to yourself, "Oh well. He still has plenty of time to grow up." This is by far the wiser of the two, because if you decide on the first, he will stumble around outside for a half hour, unable to find the leaf rake. When it finally turns up, hanging on the hook on the garage wall where it has been kept for twelve years, it will be too dark to rake leaves anyway, and all that has happened is that you have ruined a pair of stockings, and lost your temper, and now you'll have to do it yourself the next day, when today would have been far more convenient.

Sometimes they can be induced actually to make a bed, by the simple expedient of refusing to feed them any breakfast until they do. This requires enormous will power on the part of the mother, as they will now almost certainly be late for school, and if they're late to school, who'll suffer? The mother. "That lazy slob of a Mrs. Smith," everyone will say. "Wouldn't you think she could at least get her children to school on time?" So it all ends up by the mother having to drive the children to school, which is too bad, because the walk to and from school is about the only fresh air they get, and it took longer for the mother than making a couple of beds.

However, she now has to make the beds anyway, because she has gone upstairs and taken a look at them. She could leave them the way they are, and figure that as they made them, so they must lie in them, but to tell the truth the children are still grow-

ing and their bones are still soft, and she fears that if they sleep in those beds, it will permanently injure their spines. I mean, bumps and wrinkles are one thing, but when roller skates and books and globes are stirred in with the sheets and blankets. . .

If forced finally to empty an ashtray, they do it all right. Half and half. Half in the trashbasket and half on the floor. If the half on the floor is pointed out, they say, "Where? I don't see anything."

If driven to help clear the table, they do. Not one single plate is dropped, or cracked or broken. All that's dropped is two lamb chop bones, two or three corn cobs, several nice oily lettuce leaves with some pieces of tomato, and half a buttered roll—butter side down. (I *told* you you should make those children finish everything on their plates.)

Trust a child to water the plants—everything withers. Trust him to feed a pet—everyone starves. Let him wash a window—that view is gone forever.

My children washed the car once. And they did a fine thorough job of it, too. That car really shone. It was beautiful. However, unfortunately they had forgotten to close the car windows when they started, and when they finished, there was still a lot of water left in the hose, so they washed the garage, too, and then there was still more water (Kensico Reservoir holds quite a lot of water, actually) so they washed off the whole outside of the house, too, and it was really an unhappy coincidence that they forgot to close the house windows either. Then there was still more water left, so they washed off all the trees, too, and it was too bad that those careless neighbors of ours had left their car out in their driveway, because they'd forgotten to close their car windows, too.

Character building is very hard on parents. It is even sometimes hard on neighbors. It is often hard on relatives, pets, store-keepers, etc. The only people it isn't hard on are children.

Here again make use of Rule One and Rule Two (and even Rule Three when necessary). Make the damn beds yourself, empty the wastebaskets, wash the car. And then tell all the neighbors and friends that you can get to listen that your children do it *all by themselves*. Tell the children they did it all by themselves, too. They'll believe it. Let them go around telling everyone they help with all the work. It will make them feel good, and build up their egos. And all the other parents and children for miles around will feel awful. It will stir up trouble for years to *come*.

"Those marvelous Smith children," people will say. "What character! What a joy they are to their parents! They do everything around the house. They do all the snow shovelling, leaf raking, window washing, they papered their own rooms, they always get up early enough to make their own beds and keep their rooms neat ... why can't *you* be like that?"

And meanwhile you just smile modestly, and for Heaven's sake, HIDE THE GARDENER.

SIXTEEN

Reading, Writing, and Social Integration

The school plays such a vital part in the child's development and therefore in the whole future of the country that it is of the utmost importance for parents to understand its function, its aims and methods.

So much criticism has been leveled at the schools in recent years, so much controversy has raged, so many volumes have been written about teaching methods that some parents are bewildered. Should the children be taught sight reading or phonics? Are the schools placing too much emphasis on physical education or not enough? Is the discipline too strict or too lax? Are the children spending too much time in school or not enough? Should they learn geography and history or should they have social studies? Will they *never* learn to bound Manhattan Island?

(Manhattan Island is bounded on the North by the Harlem River, Spuyten Duyvil Creek and the Kill Van Kull.) How is it he's in the seventh grade and still hasn't learned that the principle product of Portugal is cork? Doesn't he know *anything* except how to dress up in cheesecloth and papier-mâché and be a frog in the school play? Aren't they ever going to teach these children any *grammar* for Heaven's sake? He doesn't even know what a semicolon is for. (What *is* a semicolon for? I feel I must have known at one time.)

The modern school educates *the whole child*. (Some of us old folks never had this advantage and as a result —see this mark on my ankle?) The school gives the child experiences in social living, the opportunity to take part in group activities with his peers, to take responsibility for the smooth functioning of this social unit. (Except for Ermentrude over there who *persists* in poking her foot into Montmorency's back.) The school provides gyms and outdoor playgrounds for the development of coordination through gross motor activity, as well as teaching the child to integrate himself into team activities. A good school provides music and art, where the child, when tired of being integrated into teams, can fully express himself as an individual with a qualified psychologist always on the alert to make sure he isn't getting *too* individual. (Like Sam who refused to draw pictures of anything but Coati mundis.) The school provides testing of the child's mental ability in order that both teachers and parents may better evaluate his potentialities in relation to other children at the same age level. (Let's face it, that kid is a dope.)

Experiences in social living notwithstanding, the

[117]

teachers are still pounding arithmetic and spelling into unwilling heads, they're still learning about the Hessians on New Year's Eve, and they still learn to sing Funiculi Funicula in three parts.

All this educational theory and all this controversy, however, overlooks the one main, vital function of the school which is really TO GET THE KIDS OUT OF THE HOUSE FROM NINE TO THREE. I cannot understand why so many parents have failed to realize this. They go around complaining about this and complaining about that, and meanwhile the thought has never struck them—where would they be without the school? When would they get the beds made? When would they get the marketing done? When would they sit down

in peace and quiet to tear their hair out? When, in fact, could they hold their PTA meetings?

Now are you going to object when they talk of raising the school tax? You see? You just didn't think it through before.

In order that the school and the parents may work together to do an optimum job on the children, many schools have a Parent Teacher Association which provides a place where mothers who have finished making their beds may go to have a cup of coffee and arrange meetings at other times where mothers may go to have a cup of coffee, at which they can decide which mothers will have the job of telephoning the other mothers to let them know when the next meeting will be held at which they may go to have a cup of coffee and elect new mothers to . . . Often, out of all this furious activity come new curtains for the school library, which is important as that is the room in which the meetings are held.

Sometimes the Parent Teacher Association holds meetings at which speakers are engaged to educate the parents to the use of phrases like "age levels," "gross motor control," "sibling rivalry," "basic insecurity," "parent resentment" and the like. The necessity for understanding these terms is self-evident. Without them, the parents could not intelligently participate in the PTA meetings.

In my own case, for example, it is extremely helpful that I have learned to say "gross motor control" because that is what my children (due to very poor heredity on their mother's side) haven't got. Otherwise I might go around saying, "They're good at reading, but they are *lousy* at baseball," and this would in no way improve their baseball. On the other hand, saying they have poor gross motor control hasn't improved their baseball either. However, as it has improved their mother's speech it is probably all worthwhile. Meanwhile, that poor physical education instructor, having failed to read Chapter X of this book which fully explains heredity and environment, is driving himself into a nervous collapse over his inability to teach my children to vault a pole or bat a ball. This is an excellent example of environment (in the person of Mr. Craik) failing to overcome heredity (in the person of me) no matter how hard it tries.

In connection with the important part played by parents in helping the schools, it is worthwhile to note that many of these interested, sincere, helpful parents accomplish a great deal by reading books on reading, whereupon they may storm these meetings demanding to know why their children are not being taught phonics, or, in some cases, demanding to know why their children are being taught phonics. This confuses the principal and the teachers who have been doggedly trying to please everybody by teaching both phonics and sight reading. Meanwhile the children, unaware of the storm raging in the library, are plugging away at, "Cat, c,u,t? C,i,t? C,o,t? C,y,t? C,e,t?" Presently, by a process of elimination they may arrive at C,a,t, and can start on k,i,t,t,e,n,s, which are sure to follow.

SEVENTEEN

The Advantages of Having Children over Hamsters or Kittens

If you have now decided that you are willing to give up certain small amenities (like sleep and money) and go on with raising children, there are, along with the hazards (ketchup, snakes and butter knives turning up in odd places) certain joys which cannot be found in raising hamsters, cats, etc.

Children around the house are a constant reminder of your own great and unexpected good luck in having finally, yourself, grown up. Daily you will be reminded how really marvelous it is that you no longer have to face the gym teacher, or sing "Poor

Punchinello" in three parts, that you no longer have to practice your piano lesson, that you don't have to worry that you won't pass your biology test. Nobody yells at you if you forget to brush your teeth, big brothers and sisters can no longer pick on you, and nobody can, ever again, chase you out of the house to get fresh air. You can frowst around and read as long as you like (having now chased your own children out of the house to get fresh air). You can shoo the children to bed early and stay up as late as you like, watching television or reading till your eyes are glassy. You can wear whatever you like, and if you feel like wearing a new dress around the house, just because you feel like it, nobody will say no.

Every morning you can watch the children drink their milk or cocoa, and you'll remember how you used to have to too, and now your lovely, hot strong coffee will taste even better. You can lecture them on the evils of tobacco while you inhale richly and luxuriously. "It's all right for *me*," you can say smugly, "*I'm* grown up."

You can make them stay home with a sitter while you go off to see any movie you like, and nobody will decide that it's "not suitable" or "not good for you."

Nobody nags you to cut your nails, brush your hair, wear your eyeglasses, wash your hands, go to bed, get up, go on errands, take vitamins, get shots, go to the dentist.

You can listen to the children playing outside with the other children in the neighborhood, and you can relax. Nobody is going to torment *you* any more because you're too fat or too thin, too tall or too short, and nobody *ever again* will make horrid rhymes about your nickname and your physical attributes.

Nobody is ever going to scold you any more if you spill things or drop things or lose things, but *you* can scold the children. They're *children.*

Best of all, as you send them forth to play things, with little exhortations about the need for bodily health and vigor, and the virtues of exercise, you can realize happily that no one will ever again try to make you play tennis, and you can curl up in a soft chair, with your spine all crooked and your chest all caved in and your muscles all limp and just enough oxygen in your blood to sustain life, and your arches comfortably flat, and you can breathe in that nice

smoky air and get yourself all full of nicotine and coal tar and caffeine and alcohol and tannic acid and you can read anything you like, even if it's absolutely stuffed with sex, *in the dark without your glasses.*

If you should ever really need exercise you can exercise your authority as a parent. "Never mind why," you can say to them, "just because I say so." (After all, if you can't exercise your authority to your children, who are you going to exercise it to? Everything else around here is so damned democratic, unless you're a policeman, you can hardly have any fun at all.)